Greek Gods and Heroes

40 inspiring icons

Sylvie Baussier & Almasty

WIDE EYED EDITIONS

Gods, Heroes, and Men

Zeus, Athena, Apollo, Oedipus and Medea... so many famous names which spark our imagination and draw us into the world of the gods and heroes of ancient Greece.

It all started over 2,500 years ago. Religion was based on the worship of numerous gods and goddesses. The Greeks built temples in their honor, made sculptures of them, recorded their history in paintings, and, of course, told stories about them. And these gods didn't just sit on their thrones in Olympus. They loved and hated each other, transformed each other's shapes, played tricks, and came down to earth to meddle in human affairs. The heroes were humans with a remarkable destiny. Often children of a god and a human, they achieved extraordinary things and were sometimes even believed to be historical figures, figures who had really existed!

The myths of their adventures teach us about Greek history. They also explain the creation of the world, the laws of nature, and the mysteries of life.

That is why for centuries, and today, they are a limitless source of inspiration for painting, literature, and film. Not just fascinating stories, the stories of Greek gods and heroes still make us dream and teach us about our world.

Contents

1

GAIA

·

2

CRONUS

·

3

ZEUS

·

4

THEMIS

·

5

HERA

6

HESTIA

·

7

PROMETHEUS

·

8

PANDORA

·

9

HADES

·

10

DEMETER

11

PERSEPHONE

·

12

APHRODITE

·

13

HEPHAESTUS

·

14

ARES

·

15

ATHENA

16

POSEIDON

·

17

APOLLO

·

18

ARTEMIS

·

19

ASCLEPIUS

·

20

HERMES

21

DIONYSUS

22

PERSEUS

23

SISYPHUS

24

OEDIPUS

25

ANTIGONE

26

HERACLES

27

ORPHEUS

28

JASON

29

MEDUSA

30

MINOTAUR

31

THESEUS

32

ARIADNE

33

PHÆDRA

34

TANTALUS

35

HELEN

36

AGAMEMNON

37

IPHIGENIA

38

ELECTRA

39

ACHILLES

40

ODYSSEUS

Gaia

Gaia is the goddess of the earth. She gave birth to the sea, the mountains, and Uranus (the starry sky). Then, with her son Uranus, king of the gods, she bore a host of extraordinary children: six Titans (who continually fought one another), six Titanesses, three Cyclopes (who each had one eye), and three Hecatonchires (who each had fifty heads and a hundred arms!). Uranus kept these children underground, but at the urging of Gaia, Cronus, the youngest Titan, rebelled and helped his brothers and sisters escape their prison, and Uranus's terrible rule.

FAMILY TREE

Sister of Chaos and Eros

Wife of Uranus

Mother to Uranus, Pontos (the sea), and the mountains

Mother, with Uranus, of six Titans and six Titanesses, three Cyclopes, and three Hecatonchires

Mother, with Pontos, of giants and nymphs

DESCENDANTS

Gaia and Uranus warned their son Cronus that if he had a son, the son would defeat him and become king in his place—the Fates had prophesied it.

CONFLICT

The tyrannical Uranus imprisoned Gaia's youngest children. Only her son Cronus volunteered to help, and he attacked his father with a sickle.

TITANS AND TITANESSES

The Titans are always ready for brutal fights, but the Titanesses don't want anything to do with them. The most famous are the Titan Cronus and the Titaness Rhea. Together, they had numerous children, who would become the Olympian gods, including Zeus, the king of the gods, who eventually took the throne from his own father.

FIRST GENERATION

Gaia, the earth, was born after Chaos, and just before Eros, love. The three are elements from nature. The children of Gaia and Uranus were the first gods to have a more or less human form.

STARRY SKY

Uranus is the sky. He covers Gaia, the earth, with his starry coat, and from this union, children are born.

SICKLE

Gaia gave her son Cronus a sickle to attack Uranus.

MOTHER

Gaia conceived numerous children, some by herself, some with Uranus, and some with Pontos.

GODDESS
of the earth

ROMAN NAME
Terra Mater

Mother Earth

Cronus

Cronus overthrew his father, Uranus, to became king of the gods, but he was as violent a king as his father had been! A prophecy foretold that one of Cronus's children would seize the throne from him, so each time his wife, Rhea, gave birth and presented their child to him, Cronus would swallow the baby. In the end, Rhea rebelled, hiding her last-born, Zeus, and replacing him with a stone wrapped in a blanket that she presented to her terrible husband. He swallowed the stone without realizing the difference, and Zeus was saved.

CONFLICT

Zeus freed his previously swallowed brothers and sisters. Together, they fought their father, Cronus, and the Titans.

HUMANS

According to Hesiod, Cronus was a good god. Under his reign, harvests grew easily and humans lived a life free from care.

A BROKEN FAMILY

Rhea wanted her cruel husband, who had swallowed their children, to die. She told her son Zeus that the Cyclopes and the Hecatonchires could help him win against Cronus. So Zeus freed them and they fought together.

A PLAY ON WORDS

Aristotle enjoyed punning on the name Cronus, as the word chronos means "time" in Greek. Thus, this violent god is also the god of time passing. But he didn't want time to pass for his children—he wanted to kill them!

FAMILY TREE

Son of Gaia and Uranus

Brother to the other Titans, the Titanesses, the Hecatonchires, and the Cyclopes

---

Husband to Rhea, a Titaness who was also his sister

Father of Hestia, Demeter, Hera, Hades, Poseidon, and Zeus

GOLDEN AGE

According to some stories, Cronus reigns over a world where humans experienced a golden age.

TERRIBLE OLD AGE

Often represented as old and ugly, Cronus lives in fear that one of his children will take the throne from him.

GOD
associated with time

ROMAN NAME
Saturn

SWADDLED STONE

Cronus didn't notice that the "baby" he swallowed was really a stone wrapped in a blanket.

A hateful god

Zeus

Zeus wasn't always king of the gods. When he was still young, he had to take power from his father, Cronus. Since then, he reigns all-powerful over the skies and Olympus, and he arbitrates any disputes that may arise between the gods. As god of nature, he has power over the human world, and sees that promises are kept and laws adhered to. He is, according to the author Homer, the "father of gods and men," with men frequently invoking his protection.

LOVERS

His third wife, Hera, who is also his sister, is known for her jealousy... but Zeus did indeed have numerous affairs with other goddesses and mortals!

LORD OF THE SKY

Once their father, Cronus, had been defeated, the Cyclopes gave each god a gift representing their divine futures. They gave Hades a helmet of invisibility, joining him forever to the kingdom of the dead. They gave Zeus thunder and lightning.

DESCENDANTS

Zeus had numerous children from his many affairs. He is father of the Muses, Heracles, Dionysus, Apollo, and Hermes.

FAMILY TREE

Son of Rhea and Cronus

Brother of Hades, Demeter, Hestia Hera, and Poseidon

Husband to Metis, mother of Athena

Husband to Themis, mother of the Horai (seasons) and the Moirai (Fates)

Husband to Hera, mother of Hebe, Eileithyia, Hephaestus, and Ares

SHAPE-SHIFTER

To get what he wants, this womanizer is capable of many tricks. He charmed Europa by turning himself into a white bull, into a swan to entice Leda, and into a shower of gold to conquer Danae. But his wife, Hera, is sometimes suspicious and comes down to earth. Occasionally, Zeus needs to change his lovers' forms—he changed Io into a heifer!

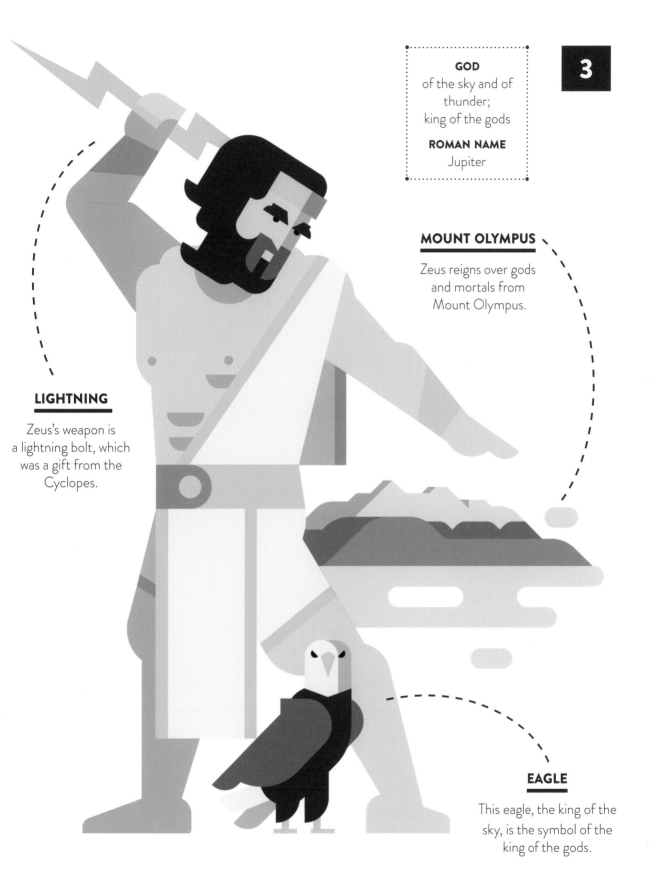

GOD
of the sky and of thunder;
king of the gods

ROMAN NAME
Jupiter

MOUNT OLYMPUS

Zeus reigns over gods and mortals from Mount Olympus.

LIGHTNING

Zeus's weapon is a lightning bolt, which was a gift from the Cyclopes.

EAGLE

This eagle, the king of the sky, is the symbol of the king of the gods.

King of the gods

Themis

Themis is a goddess and sister to the Titans. By marrying Zeus, she ensured that she remained important when he took power. Zeus had been married to another goddess, Metis, but after an oracle prophesied that her unborn son would become king of the gods in his father's place, Zeus ate her. Themis, goddess of justice, has powers of divination and inspires wisdom in humans. She stayed on Mount Olympus even when Zeus later married his sister Hera.

HUMANS

Her daughters the Horai (Justice, Discipline, and Peace) watch over the seasons and also justice among men.

FAMILY TREE

Daughter of Uranus and Gaia

Sister to the Titans (she's one of the Titanesses)

Zeus's second wife, after Metis and before Hera

Mother of the Horai, Moirai, and Astraea

CONFLICT

When Zeus fought the giants, Themis advised him to protect himself with Amalthea's skin. Amalthea was the goat who had fed him when he was a baby.

TELL THE FUTURE

Well before Apollo, Themis prophesied the future at Delphi. She founded the oracle there. She sat on a tripod, as Pythia later would, and answered questions that humans came to ask her. They then had to interpret her often-confusing responses!

THE MOIRAI

Atropos, Clotho, and Lachesis are the daughters of Themis and Zeus. Known as the Moirai, or the Fates, they are the mistresses of human destiny: one spins the thread of life, the second measures it, and the third cuts the thread when it's time for death.

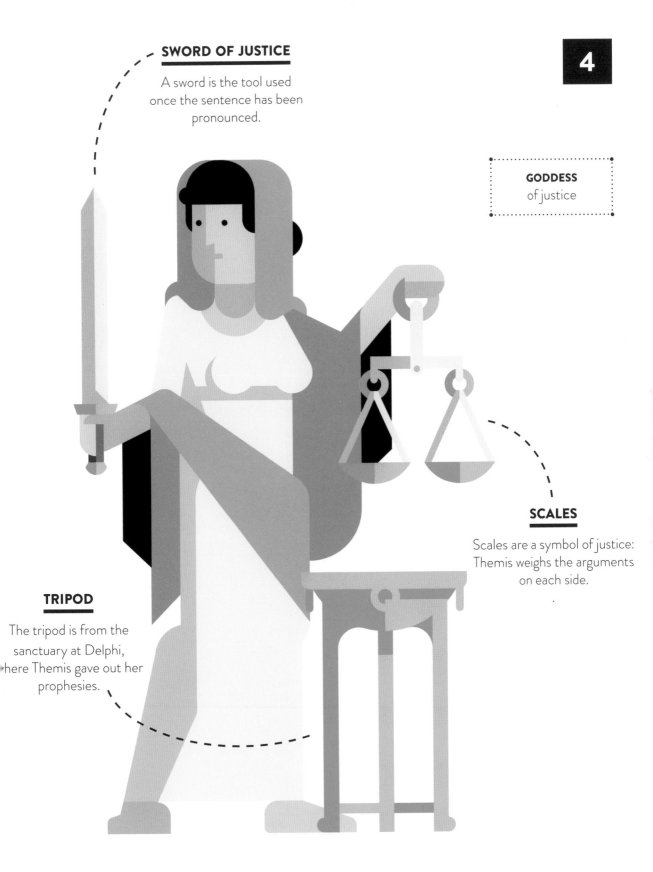

SWORD OF JUSTICE

A sword is the tool used once the sentence has been pronounced.

GODDESS
of justice

SCALES

Scales are a symbol of justice: Themis weighs the arguments on each side.

TRIPOD

The tripod is from the sanctuary at Delphi, where Themis gave out her prophesies.

Guardian of laws

Hera

Hera is married to Zeus, king of the gods. Her husband's constant infidelity makes her fiercely jealous. However, it isn't Zeus who bears the brunt of this jealousy, but those whom he seduces and the children born of these unions. To obtain what he desired from the beautiful Alcmene, the faithful wife of Amphitryon, Zeus took on her husband's appearance. From their union, Heracles was born. Hera punished this innocent child for his divine father's wrongdoing by giving him twelve seemingly impossible tasks.

IO'S TRANSFORMATION

A nymph named Io was courted by Zeus—and Hera knew all about it. The king of the gods had just enough time to change Io into a white heifer, which Hera then begged for as a gift and asked Argus to guard.

DESCENDANTS

Eileithyia, daughter of Hera and Zeus, presides over childbirth. Without her, no woman can give birth.

FAMILY TREE

Daughter of Cronus and Rhea

Wife of Zeus, who is also her brother

Mother to Eileithyia, Hephaestus, Hebe, and Ares

CONFLICT

Hera spends an enormous amount of time spying on Zeus. As soon as she sees her husband wooing a beautiful woman—whether a goddess or a mortal—Hera wages war against her.

WANDERING LETO

Leto, daughter of the Titans, was pregnant by Zeus. Hera forbade all lands from allowing her to give birth. But she wasn't able to stop the birth of Leto's twins, Apollo and Artemis.

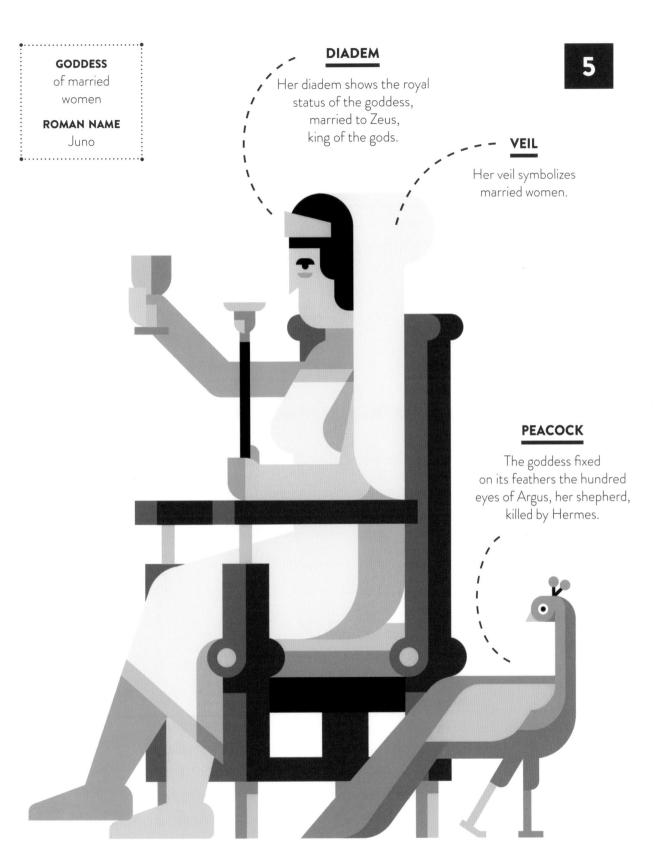

GODDESS
of married
women

ROMAN NAME
Juno

DIADEM
Her diadem shows the royal
status of the goddess,
married to Zeus,
king of the gods.

VEIL
Her veil symbolizes
married women.

PEACOCK
The goddess fixed
on its feathers the hundred
eyes of Argus, her shepherd,
killed by Hermes.

Jealous goddess

Hestia

Hestia, Rhea's firstborn child, was also the first to be swallowed by her father, Cronus, who feared being deposed by his descendants. Thanks to her brother Zeus, the goddess was finally spat out, alive and kicking. Zeus is then king of the gods and allows her to remain forever a virgin, and she refused the advances of Apollo and Poseidon. She lives peacefully on Olympus. Her home is there, but also with all humans and in all cities, as she is the goddess of hearth and home.

FAMILY TREE

Daughter of Cronus and Rhea

Sister to Poseidon, Hades, Zeus, Hera, and Demeter

WORSHIP

In every house, rich or poor, and in many temples, even when they are dedicated to another god, Hestia is worshipped.

DESCENDANTS

Hestia watches over pregnant women and babies, those who need the most protection in the home.

THE SACRED FIRE

The fire was the symbol and the heart of the home. When the Greeks left their city to set up a new one, they took some of their sacred fire with them, and it is Hestia they are taking with them. The fire of Hestia is also used during sacrifices.

WELCOMED

When Heracles died, he was welcomed to Olympus with great ceremony by Hestia. Thanks to her, he reconciled with Hera during a ritual that reenacted the scene of his birth. Without Hestia, mistress of the home, this reconciliation would not have been possible.

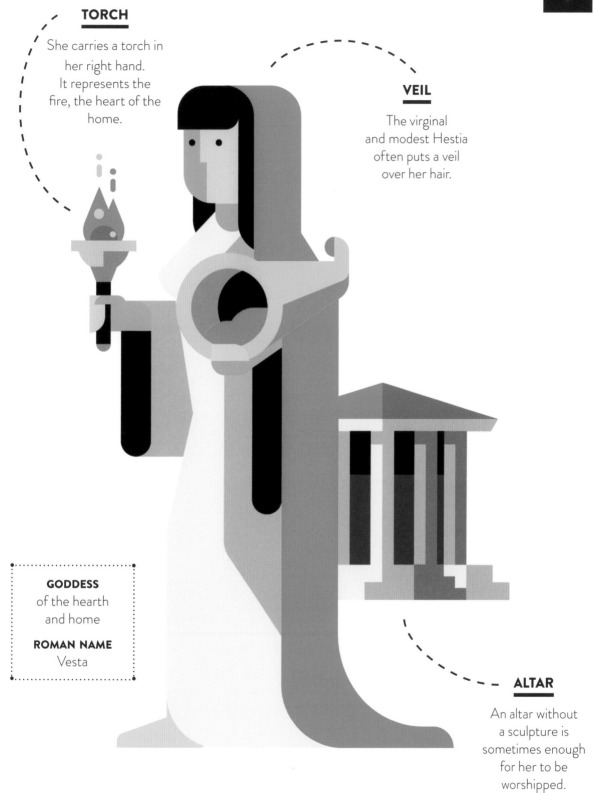

TORCH

She carries a torch in her right hand. It represents the fire, the heart of the home.

VEIL

The virginal and modest Hestia often puts a veil over her hair.

GODDESS
of the hearth and home

ROMAN NAME
Vesta

ALTAR

An altar without a sculpture is sometimes enough for her to be worshipped.

Goddess of the hearth

Prometheus

The cunning Prometheus thinks before he acts, which is, in fact, what his name means. His brother Epimetheus, on the other hand, acts before he thinks.

Like Zeus, Prometheus is the son of a Titan. Their view of humans, however, differs. Zeus expects submission and honor; Prometheus is their ally. During a sacrifice, he separated a bull into two parts. One part consisted of the bones, covered with beautiful white fat, while the other part was the edible meat, hidden under the unappetizing-looking skin and stomach. He asked Zeus to choose between the two parts. The king of the gods chose the better-looking pile—and it was inedible. He had been tricked and was furious.

MEN AND FIRE

In revenge for Prometheus's trickery, Zeus took fire away from humans. But how could they eat if they couldn't cook food? Prometheus went to Olympus, stole some fire from the sun, hid it in a fennel stalk, and brought it back to the humans.

FAMILY TREE

Son of Iapetus the Titan, and Clymene, daughter of the ocean

Brother to Epimetheus and Atlas

Cousin to Zeus

Husband to Celaeno

Father of Deucalion, Lycos, and Chimaerea

CONFLICT

Zeus chained Prometheus to a rock and continually inflicted torture on him. Zeus finally allowed Heracles to rescue Prometheus.

MORTAL OR IMMORTAL?

After Heracles saved him, Prometheus met the centaur Chiron, who, injured by one of Heracles's arrows, was badly suffering. In order to die, he had to give someone his immortality. Prometheus accepted and became immortal in his place.

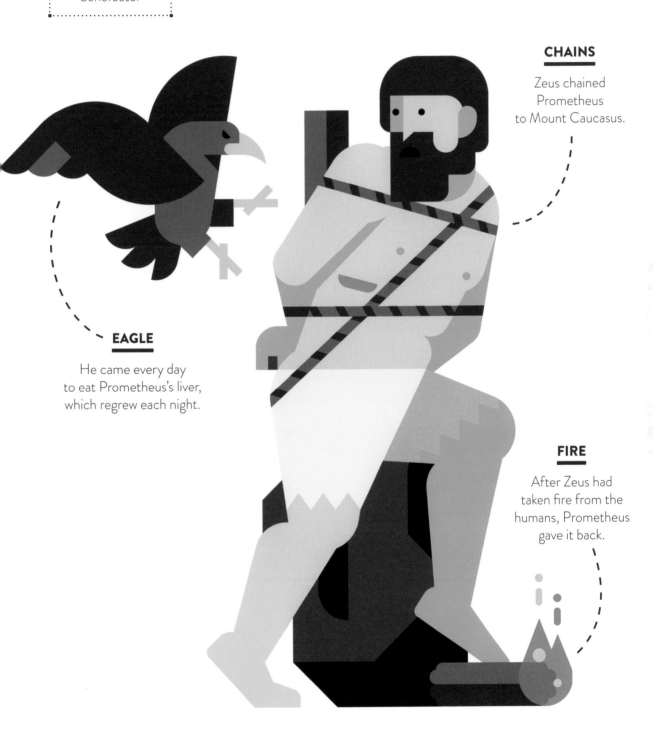

TITAN
human
benefactor

CHAINS

Zeus chained
Prometheus
to Mount Caucasus.

EAGLE

He came every day
to eat Prometheus's liver,
which regrew each night.

FIRE

After Zeus had
taken fire from the
humans, Prometheus
gave it back.

Ally of the mortals

Pandora

Zeus wanted to punish the humans who had defied him when they accepted meat and fire from Prometheus. He ordered the god Hephaestus to mold a being out of earth. This was Pandora, the first woman. The goddess Aphrodite gave her beauty and the art of seduction; Peitho, an Oceanid, gave her the art of persuasion; Apollo, that of music; and Hermes, the gift of lying. Pandora had a jar containing evil and misery. When she came down to the human world, she brought the jar with her—and no one could resist her charms.

POISONED GIFT

Once upon a time, men lived with gods in a golden age where nobody needed to work. But when they opposed Zeus, he sealed their fate by sending them the beautiful Pandora.

FAMILY TREE

Created by the gods, made by Hephaestus, helped by Athena

Wife of Epimetheus

Mother to Pyrrha

WARNING

Prometheus had warned his brother Epimetheus that if Zeus gave him a present, he was not to accept it. But when the king of the gods sent him Pandora, Epimetheus, captivated by her beauty, forgot everything his brother had said and married her.

HUMANS

Zeus gave Pandora a jar that she was not to open. But her curiosity got the better of her. Death, disease, sadness, and all the evils of human existence escaped into the world.

DEED

Pandora quickly closed the jar. But all the evils from the jar had spread over the earth. The only thing left in the jar was hope, which allowed humans to endure such evil.

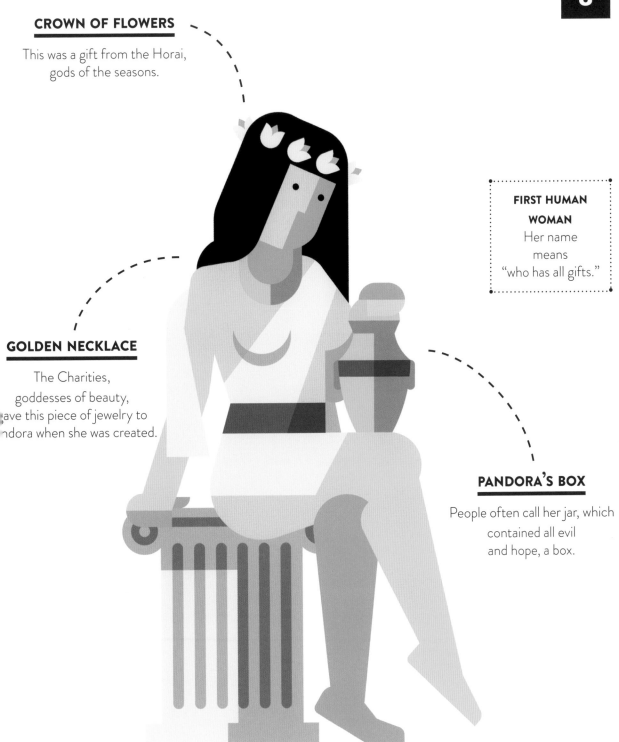

CROWN OF FLOWERS

This was a gift from the Horai, gods of the seasons.

FIRST HUMAN WOMAN
Her name means "who has all gifts."

GOLDEN NECKLACE

The Charities, goddesses of beauty, gave this piece of jewelry to Pandora when she was created.

PANDORA'S BOX

People often call her jar, which contained all evil and hope, a box.

The first woman

Hades

Hades is the brother of Zeus and the other Olympians. But he wasn't as lucky as them. Zeus ordered him to reign over hell and stop the dead from leaving. It wasn't a fun job! Hades, with no choice in the matter, had to become king of a gray underground world. His name, which could mean "the invisible" was supposed to bring bad luck. So as not to have to say it, the Greeks sometimes called him Pluto, "the rich." It is indeed under the earth where you find the "riches" of iron and silver, and where plants put down their roots.

WORSHIP

Hades frightens and worries humans. There are virtually no temples consecrated to him.

THE UNDERWORLD

Hades doesn't treat all the dead in the same way. Those who offended the gods endured punishment in an area of hell called Tartarus. Good men and heroes go to the Elysian Fields, a paradise of happiness.

LOVERS

Hades, tired of being alone, kidnapped his niece Kore and married her under the name of Persephone.

FAMILY TREE

Son of Cronus and Rhea

Brother to Zeus, Demetrius, Hera, Hades, Poseidon, and Hestia

Husband to Persephone

CROSSING THE STYX

The dead have to take Charon's ferry to cross the river Styx and find rest in the underworld. Otherwise, their soul must wander. The dead are buried with a coin in their mouth in order to pay Charon for his services.

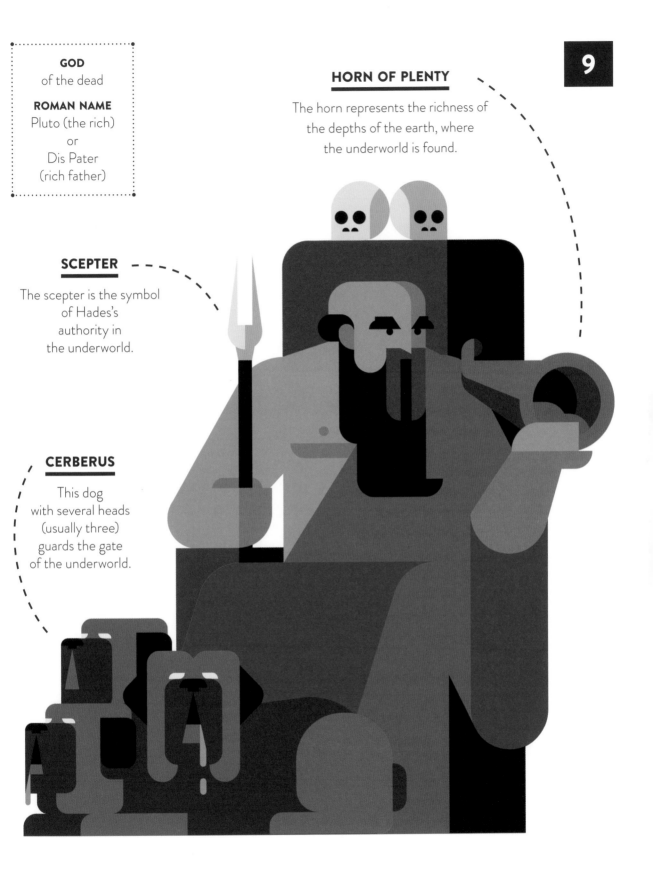

GOD
of the dead
ROMAN NAME
Pluto (the rich)
or
Dis Pater
(rich father)

HORN OF PLENTY
The horn represents the richness of
the depths of the earth, where
the underworld is found.

SCEPTER
The scepter is the symbol
of Hades's
authority in
the underworld.

CERBERUS
This dog
with several heads
(usually three)
guards the gate
of the underworld.

King of hell

HUMANS

The Greeks are essentially an agricultural people, which is why they adore Demeter, who is supposed to have saved them from famine.

Demeter

Demeter, goddess of the harvest, had a child with Zeus. When Kore was a young woman, she was playing with her friends, when she suddenly disappeared under the ground. For nine days, her mother looked for her. At Eleusis, Demeter learned that Hades had kidnapped Kore. Demeter vowed not to carry out her duties as goddess of the harvest until she found her daughter. Nature suffered, and nothing would grow. Zeus had to intervene. He decided that for half the year, Kore would come back to live on earth.

WORSHIP

Demeter is worshipped at Eleusis, near Athens, in secret ceremonies called "the mysteries," which celebrate the cycles of nature.

FAMILY TREE

Daughter of Cronus and Rhea

Sister to Zeus, Hades, Hestia, Poseidon, and Hera

Mother of Kore, who became queen of the underworld under the name Persephone

TRIPTOLEMUS

At Eleusis, Demeter was very kindly welcomed by Celeus, the king of the city. To thank him, she taught the young prince Triptolemus how to grow wheat. Then she sent him on a chariot drawn by winged dragons to go and teach others.

THE SEASONS

While Kore is under the ground, in the underworld with her husband, Hades, Demeter despairs and the earth is cold. This is autumn and winter. When her daughter returns, she is happy! Nature blooms again, and we have spring and summer.

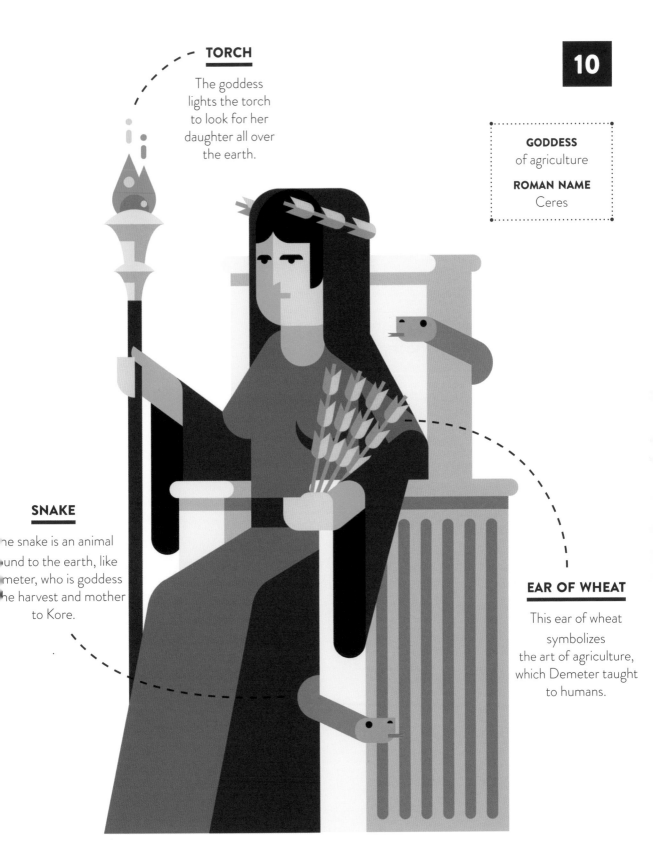

TORCH

The goddess lights the torch to look for her daughter all over the earth.

GODDESS
of agriculture

ROMAN NAME
Ceres

SNAKE

he snake is an animal und to the earth, like meter, who is goddess he harvest and mother to Kore.

EAR OF WHEAT

This ear of wheat symbolizes the art of agriculture, which Demeter taught to humans.

A mother in pain

Persephone

LOVERS

In the underworld, Hades offered his niece Kore a pomegranate, which the young girl accepted. She did not know that this would condemn her to stay there and marry him.

The young goddess Kore was very attached to her mother, Demeter. Her uncle Hades, who was tired of being alone in the underworld, fell in love with her. One day, when she was picking flowers with her nymph friends in Sicily, she wandered off. Then there was a roar, and the ground opened—and Kore disappeared with a cry of terror. Demeter heard it and knew that something terrible had happened to her daughter. From then on, Kore was a prisoner in the underworld. Hades renamed her Persephone.

ZEUS THE ACCOMPLICE

Zeus had come up with the scheme with Hades. But he had to give in to Demeter, who wanted to see her daughter. If Demeter, goddess of the harvest, refused to carry out her role, nature would suffer. So Persephone was allowed to return for half the year.

DEATH

As the queen of the underworld, Persephone orders the coming of the dead. Hermes, as a good messenger, carries out her orders.

GOODNESS

Sometimes Persephone is merciful. She allowed Orpheus to take his wife, Euridice, out of the underworld, on the condition that he didn't look back when they left.

FAMILY TREE

Daughter of Zeus and Demeter

Niece to Zeus, Hades, Hestia, Poseidon, and Hera

Wife of Hades

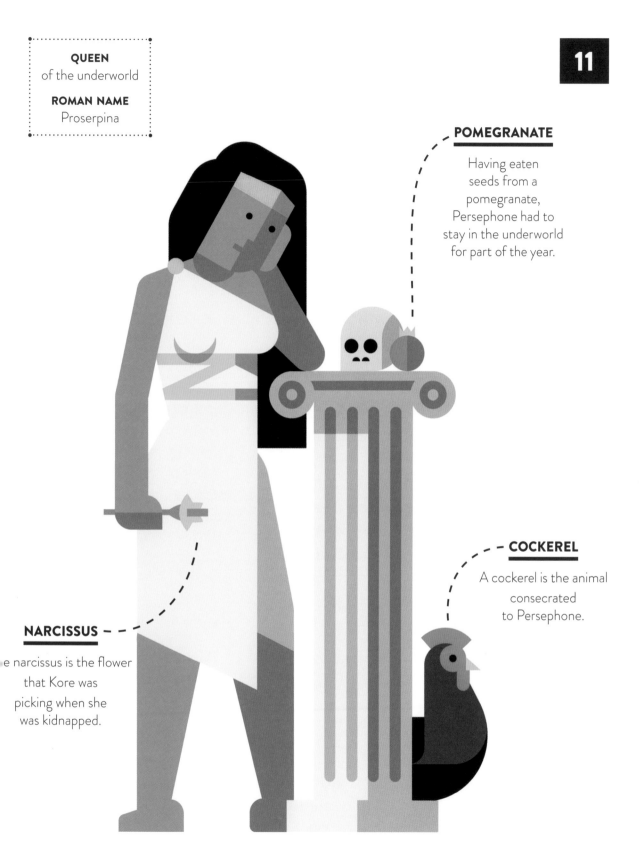

QUEEN
of the underworld

ROMAN NAME
Proserpina

POMEGRANATE

Having eaten seeds from a pomegranate, Persephone had to stay in the underworld for part of the year.

COCKEREL

A cockerel is the animal consecrated to Persephone.

NARCISSUS

e narcissus is the flower that Kore was picking when she was kidnapped.

A double life

Aphrodite

Aphrodite is the daughter of Zeus and the goddess Dione, according to Homer. But another tradition has her as a much older goddess: Uranus, the sky, was with Gaia, the earth, but Gaia couldn't stand her violent husband any longer. Cronus, their son, flew to his mother's aid. He cut off his father's genitals, which fell into the sea and fertilized it. Aphrodite came out of the water, with the features of a beautiful young goddess. Her charm worked its magic on numerous gods and even began the terrible Trojan War.

A FORCED MARRIAGE

Hephaestus, the god of blacksmiths, fell madly in love with Aphrodite. But she wasn't at all interested in the ugly god with a limp. However, she had to marry him, per Zeus's orders. But this didn't stop her from spending time with the handsome Ares...

FAMILY TREE

Wife of Hephaestus

Aphrodite had many lovers—the most famous was Ares, god of war

Mother of Aeneas, the mythical ancestor of the Romans

LOVERS

The sun surprised Aphrodite when she was in the arms of Ares, her lover, with whom she had spent the night. He told Hephaestus, who trapped them in a magic net.

FOR TROY

Eris, goddess of Discord, promised a golden apple to the most beautiful goddess. Paris, who had to pick, chose Aphrodite above Hera and Athena. From then on, Eris protected this Trojan prince and his people against the Greeks.

DOVE

Aphrodite is often represented with a dove, her favorite animal.

GODDESS
of love
and of beauty

ROMAN NAME
Venus

A GOLDEN APPLE

A golden apple was the prize for the beauty contest that Aphrodite won over all the other goddesses.

EROS

According to some versions of the myth, Eros, the god of love, is the son of Aphrodite.

The most beautiful of goddesses

Hephaestus

LOVERS

Hephaestus, on Zeus's orders, used earth to create Pandora, the first woman, who played the role of seductor.

Hephaestus is the ugliest god. Hera, his mother, found him so revolting at birth that she threw him out of Olympus, which injured him and gave him a limp. The child was welcomed into the ocean by Thetis and Eurynome, who raised him in a cave. When he had grown, Hephaestus learned to be a blacksmith and mixed magic with his art. He gave a superb golden throne to Hera, who, flattered, sat on it, but couldn't get up again. Hephaestus freed her on the condition that she did not return to Olympus.

ZEUS'S ALLY

Hephaestus helped Zeus on several occasions. He fought by his side against the giants and killed one of them, Clytius, with a massive blow. On another occasion, he freed Zeus from terrible suffering by splitting open his head. Out came Athena.

FAMILY TREE

Son of Zeus and Hera (or Hera alone, depending on the version)

Brother to Eileithyia, Hebe, and Ares

Husband of Aphrodite

Father of Palaemon (an Argonaut) and Ardalos (a sculptor)

HUMANS

When the Greeks heard rumblings underground, they thought it was Hephaestus working in his forge at the bottom of a volcano.

THE MAGIC NET

Hephaestus trapped his unfaithful wife, Aphrodite, and Ares in a net he had made of delicate but indestructible chains so he could bring them to Olympus and the gods could come and mock the two lovers.

PILEUS

The pileus was the hat worn by the infantry.

HAMMER AND ANVIL

With these tools, the god of blacksmiths works metal.

GOD
of fire
and the forge

ROMAN NAME
Vulcan

MULE

It was on a mule that Hephaestus returned to Olympus.

The ugly god

Ares was humiliated when he and
Aphrodite were brought to Olympus
trapped in a net. He ran away to Thrace.
And that was the end of the affair!

Ares

This god enjoys the noise and rage of battle. Ares intervenes in human disputes without thinking about who is right and who is wrong. In the Trojan War, he often switched sides, sometimes fighting on the side of the Trojans and sometimes with the Greeks, who had the city of Troy under siege. He fights on foot, or on a chariot pulled by four horses. With his great stature, he towers above any scene. When he is not at war, or in the arms of beautiful Aphrodite, he lives in Thrace, a wild region, which suits his character.

CONFLICT

Ares is not always victorious. He was hurt on the battlefield at Troy, by Athena, who was made invisible, thanks to Hades's helmet. Ares had to go to Mount Olympus to be healed.

DEFENDING HIS DAUGHTER

During the Trojan War, the Amazons came to provide manpower (rather, womanpower) to the Trojans. One of them—Ares's daughter Penthesilea—was wounded by Achilles, and died. Ares wanted to save her, but Zeus stopped him. Even the gods have to obey the Fates.

FEARSOME SONS

Ares's children were as violent as he was. His son Diomedes of Thrace took pleasure in feeding humans to his mares. Heracles eventually captured the horses and fed their master to them.

FAMILY TREE

Son of Zeus and Hera

Brother to Eileithyia, Hebe, and Hephaestus

Father of Eros, Harmony, and Penthesiles (amongst others)

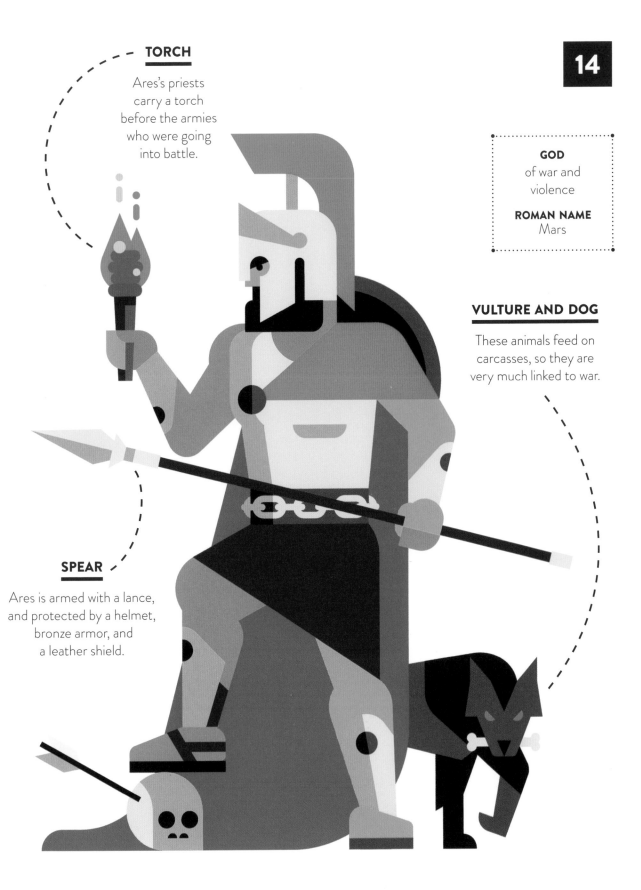

TORCH

Ares's priests carry a torch before the armies who were going into battle.

GOD
of war and violence

ROMAN NAME
Mars

VULTURE AND DOG

These animals feed on carcasses, so they are very much linked to war.

SPEAR

Ares is armed with a lance, and protected by a helmet, bronze armor, and a leather shield.

The war-loving god

HUMANS

During the Trojan War, Athena protected the Greeks, especially Odysseus. Poseidon, on the other hand, pursued Odysseus.

Athena

Athena was born as an adult wearing armor: she has always been ready for combat! She combines wisdom with desire for war. She taught humans the art forms of pottery and weaving. When competing with Poseidon to be the protector of a large city in Greece, she offered the gift of an olive tree and showed the city's inhabitants how to extract olive oil from it. The Olympians declared her the victor and the city was named Athens, in honor of the goddess of war and wisdom.

WORSHIP

The Panathenaea is a festival that happens in the summer in Athens. There are processions, sport competitions, and music.

BIRTH

Zeus learned that if his partner, Metis, had a child, the child would depose him. So he ate the pregnant Metis. Soon, suffering from a terrible headache, Zeus begged Hephaestus to split his skull open. Athena sprung out with a terrible war cry.

ARACHNE

A young girl named Arachne claimed to be a better weaver than Athena. So they held a competition. But Athena didn't wait to be judged...she destroyed the work of her rival and then transformed the girl into a spider spinning her web.

FAMILY TREE

Daughter of Zeus and Metis

She refused to marry, but brought up Erichthonius, who was half man, half snake, son of the earth and Hephaestus

GODDESS
of wisdom
and war

ROMAN NAME
Minerva

HELMET
Athena came out of Zeus's
head fully armed.

OWL

A silent and
often-still bird, this
little owl symbolizes
wisdom.

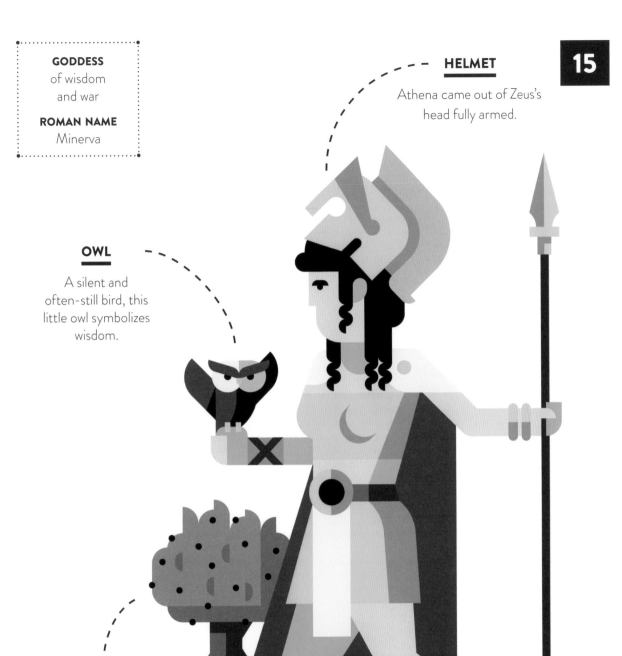

OLIVE TREE

This tree
was given to the
Athenians to give
them fruits
and oil.

The protector of the Greeks

Poseidon

There are numerous temples dedicated to Poseidon on coasts and capes. He is also worshipped at Thessaly, Athens, and Corinth.

Poseidon is protector of the waters, notably the Aegean Sea. He wanted to reign over a city, but each time there is a competition for a city, it is his divine opponent who is victorious: Athena at Athens and Hera at Argos, for example. Furious, Poseidon brought a drought upon the entire Argolid region. Amymone, a Danaide whom he loved, made him provide drinking water again. The god of the sea was as unlucky at Corinth, where Helios, the god of the sun, ultimately became the city's protector.

FATHER AND SON

Poseidon had several children, including the Cyclops Polyphemus. When Odysseus, blinded Polyphemus on his way home from Troy, Poseidon was furious and did all he could to delay the return of the hero to Ithaca, sending terrible winds across the sea.

FAMILY TREE

Son of Cronus and Rhea

Brother to Zeus, Hades, Hera, Poseidon, and Hestia

Husband to Amphitrite

He had numerous children, including Triton, Pegasus, and Polyphemus

HUMANS

The god built a huge wall around Troy to protect the city from the Greeks. But when the king Laomedon refused to pay, Poseidon took the side of the Greeks.

STRANGE STEEDS

To cross the seas, Poseidon has a bronze chariot that moves on the waves. This chariot is pulled by animals with the top half of a horse and the bottom half of a sea snake.

GOD
of the sea
and lakes

ROMAN NAME
Neptune

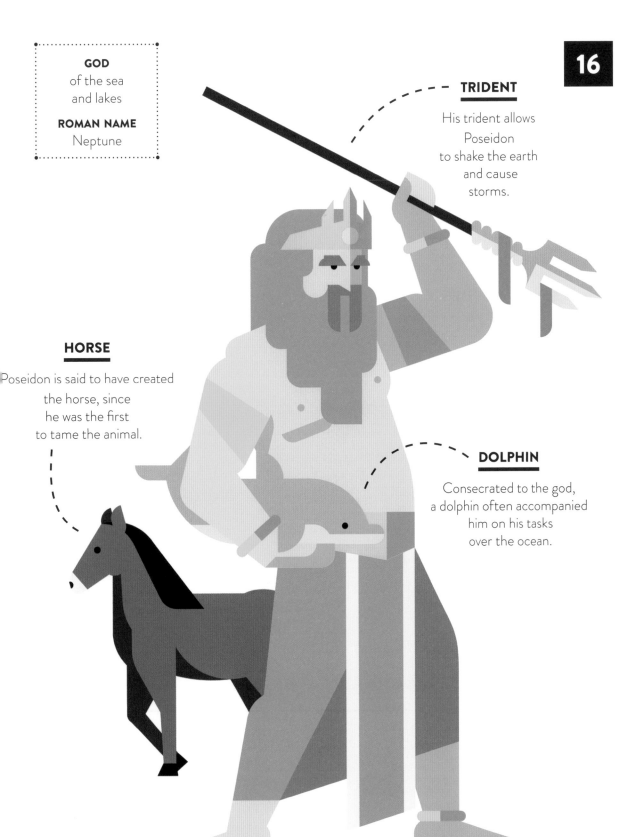

TRIDENT

His trident allows
Poseidon
to shake the earth
and cause
storms.

HORSE

Poseidon is said to have created
the horse, since
he was the first
to tame the animal.

DOLPHIN

Consecrated to the god,
a dolphin often accompanied
him on his tasks
over the ocean.

Ruler of the seas

Apollo

Apollo is so handsome! He has long curls, sparkling eyes, and an athletic build. Hera had tried to prevent his birth, because Apollo was the result of an affair between her husband, Zeus, and Leto, but she didn't manage it. Apollo is extremely talented: no one plays the lyre better than he does, and he can foretell the future. He is as brilliant at reciting poetry as he is at fighting. Apollo is also a sun god. He and his twin sister, Artemis, protect their mother when she is in danger.

FORBIDDEN BIRTH

Hera forbade all lands from allowing pregnant Leto to come to them to give birth. Finally, a small floating island accepted her, a woman who had been rejected everywhere else. Leto gave birth to a daughter, Artemis, who immediately helped her to give birth to a son, Apollo.

CONFLICT

Apollo couldn't bear it that the satyr Marsyas claimed to be the best lyre player. He challenged him, beat him, and then hanged him! Marsyas was then turned into a rushing river.

FAMILY TREE

Son of Zeus and Leto

Brother to Artemis

Linked to the nymph Cyrene and to numerous other women and goddesses, notably Coronis

Father with Cyrene to Aristaeus and numerous other children, notably Asclepius

WORSHIP

The Pythia serves as the oracle at the Temple of Apollo in Delphi. Sitting on her tripod, she can predict the future for humans, but in ways that are difficult to interpret.

THWARTED LOVE

Apollo was not always happily in love! The nymph Daphne chose to be transformed into a laurel tree rather than give in to his advances. Coronis, who was pregnant by Apollo, preferred a mere mortal. Apollo took revenge on her by having Artemis kill her!

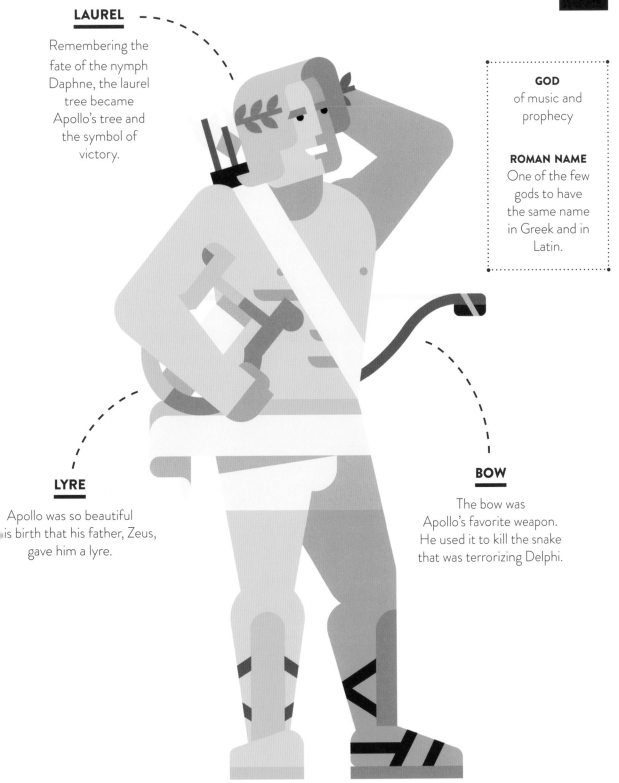

LAUREL

Remembering the fate of the nymph Daphne, the laurel tree became Apollo's tree and the symbol of victory.

GOD
of music and prophecy

ROMAN NAME
One of the few gods to have the same name in Greek and in Latin.

LYRE

Apollo was so beautiful is birth that his father, Zeus, gave him a lyre.

BOW

The bow was Apollo's favorite weapon. He used it to kill the snake that was terrorizing Delphi.

The sun god

Artemis

Artemis is a young goddess who will always be a virgin. When a human or a giant surprises her when she is naked, Artemis becomes pitiless. Actaeon was one who faced her wrath. The hunter couldn't help but admire the goddess, who was bathing in a stream. She transformed Actaeon into a stag and turned his own dogs against him. On another occasion, she sent a scorpion to sting Orion, a giant who had tried to seduce her. In thanks for this service, she placed the animal in the sky and turned him into a constellation.

CONFLICT

When Niobe, a mortal, dared to mock Artemis's mother, Leto, Artemis killed Niobe's seven daughters in retaliation.

WORSHIP

Artemis is worshipped in Tauris, where the high priestess Iphigenia has to kill those who have been shipwrecked. At Ephesus, she is worshipped as goddess of fertility.

FAMILY TREE

Daughter of Zeus and the Titaness Leto

A PROUD GODDESS

To avenge herself against King Agamemnon, who had killed one of her sacred deer, Artemis demanded the sacrifice of Iphigenia, the ruler's daughter. But at the last moment, the goddess saved Iphigenia, putting a deer in her place.

ARTEMIS'S STAG

One of the labors of Heracles was to take a stag with golden antlers, sacred to Artemis, to his cousin Eurystheus. Unable to catch up with it, the hero ended up killing it, and only just escaped from the goddess's anger.

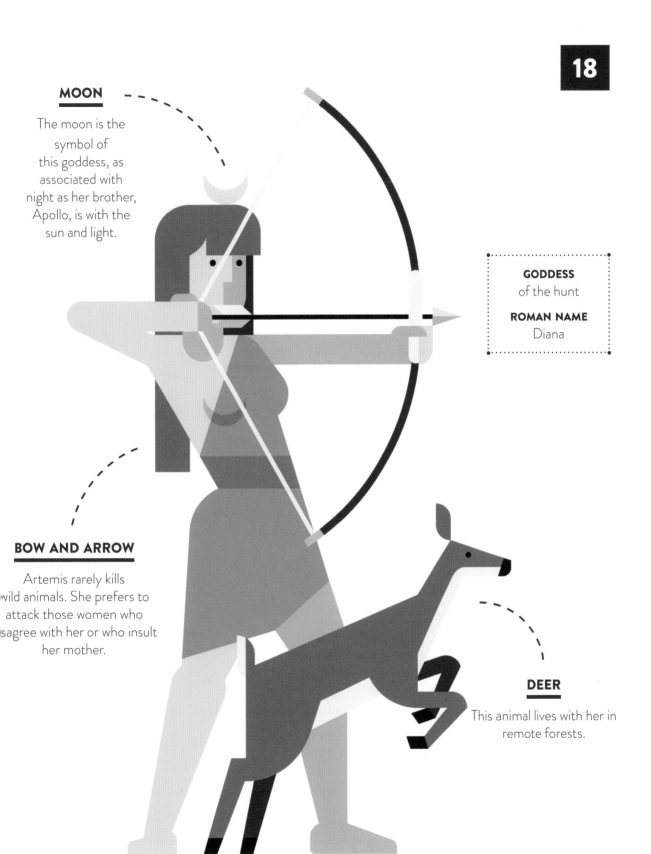

MOON

The moon is the symbol of this goddess, as associated with night as her brother, Apollo, is with the sun and light.

GODDESS
of the hunt

ROMAN NAME
Diana

BOW AND ARROW

Artemis rarely kills wild animals. She prefers to attack those women who disagree with her or who insult her mother.

DEER

This animal lives with her in remote forests.

Chaste and wild goddess

Asclepius

WORSHIP

The sanctuary at Epidaurus is dedicated to this god. Ill people purify themselves, then sleep among the snakes. Priests interpret divine dreams here.

The princess Coronis had a son with Apollo named Asclepius. The god of prophecy had to leave her, so he asked a white crow to keep an eye on the beautiful princess. However, Coronis fell in love with a mortal, Ischys. Apollo, mad with rage, scorched the crow's feathers black and sent Artemis to kill the unfaithful Coronis. But Asclepius was saved. The child was taught by Chiron and received a precious gift from Athena: Medusa's blood. This blood can poison, or bring back to life. With it, Asclepius had limitless power.

CHIRON

Chiron is a kindly centaur. with the body of a horse and the chest of a man. He taught Asclepius to become a healer. Asclepius's sons, Machaon and Podalirius, also learned how to heal, becoming doctors to the Greeks in the Trojan War.

DEATH

Zeus struck Asclepius with lightning and turned him into a constellation, as being able to make men live again upsets the natural order of things.

MEDICINE OR MAGIC

Asclepius is the god of doctors. Some practitioners like Hippocrat asked sick people questions, observed their symptoms, and prescribed remedies. Others were charlatans who claimed to heal with the help of magic.

FAMILY TREE

Son of Apollo and Coronis

Husband to Lampetia

Father of two boys, Podalirius and Machaon, and three daughters, Panacea, Iaso, and Hygieia

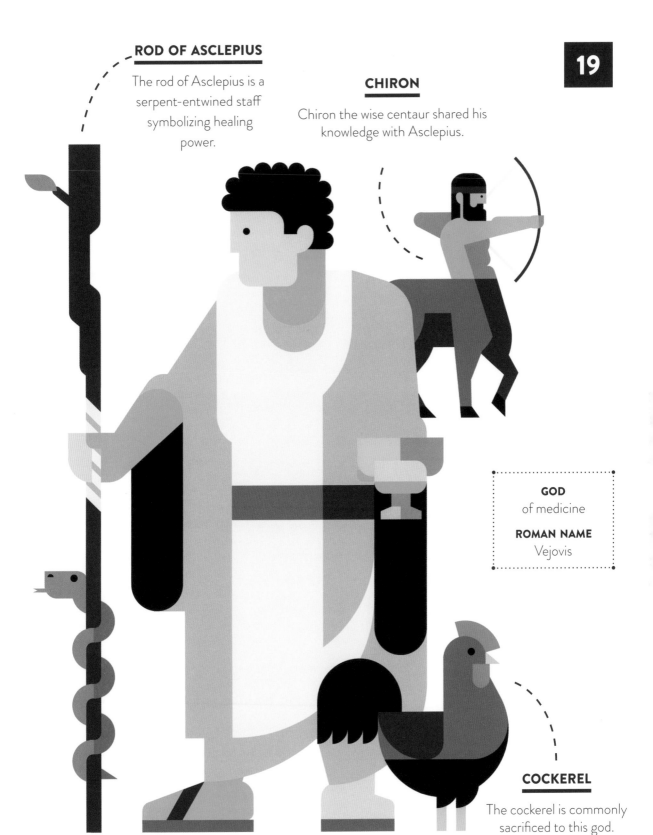

ROD OF ASCLEPIUS

The rod of Asclepius is a serpent-entwined staff symbolizing healing power.

CHIRON

Chiron the wise centaur shared his knowledge with Asclepius.

GOD
of medicine

ROMAN NAME
Vejovis

COCKEREL

The cockerel is commonly sacrificed to this god.

The god of healing

DEATH

Hermes takes the dead to the underworld and makes sure they cross the river Styx on Charon's ferry.

Hermes

From birth, Hermes was lively, energetic, and cunning. While his mother thought he was asleep, the god, still just a baby, took off all his swaddling clothes and flew off to join a part of the flock that Apollo was supposed to be watching over. He made certain that the beasts would leave no tracks by attaching branches to their tails, took them across Greece, made a sacrifice to the Olympians, and got back to bed before dawn. Zeus, amused by his son, made him his messenger. Hermes features in numerous myths as a side character.

DEED

Hermes takes messages from the king of the gods, notably to the underworld. Zeus also commanded he kill Argus, who was supposed to be watching Io, and that he help Dionysus escape Hera's wrath.

INVENTOR

Hermes invented astronomy, the alphabet, and the flute. He gave the flute to his half brother, Apollo, in exchange for lessons on the art of divination, and he too became a master of prophecy.

ON THE HEROES' SIDE

Hermes helped numerous heroes: he gave Perseus Hades's helmet to make him invisible to Gorgon eyes; he saved Heracles, who had gone to fight Medusa's ghost in the Underworld; and he assisted Odysseus, a victim of Circe's magic.

FAMILY TREE

Son of Zeus and Maia, a Pleiad

Father of Pan, whom he had by a nymph, and Hermaphrodite, whom he had by Aphrodite
He also has other children

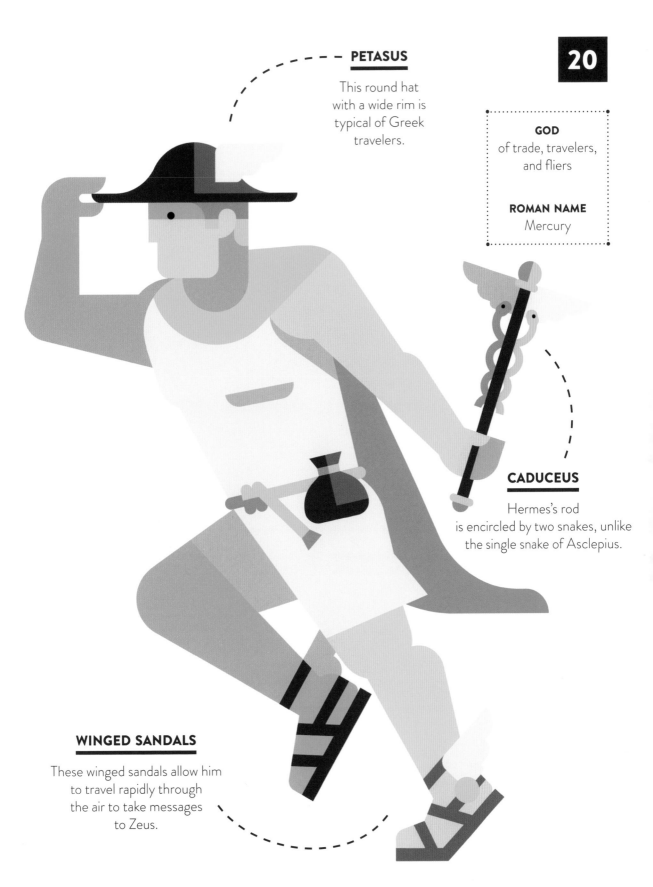

20

PETASUS
This round hat with a wide rim is typical of Greek travelers.

GOD
of trade, travelers, and fliers

ROMAN NAME
Mercury

CADUCEUS
Hermes's rod is encircled by two snakes, unlike the single snake of Asclepius.

WINGED SANDALS
These winged sandals allow him to travel rapidly through the air to take messages to Zeus.

Zeus's messenger

Dionysus

Dionysus was plagued by violence even before he was born. Hera, knowing that Zeus loved Semele, suggested that Semele demand Zeus prove his divinity by appearing before her in his true person. Of course, the beauty could not withstand the sight of the king of the gods in all his splendor, surrounded by lightning bolts. She died, struck by lightning. Zeus just had time to save his son, Dionysus, who was still in his mother's womb. Hera continued to follow the child, attempting to kill him and drive him mad.

DESCENDANTS

With Semele killed by lightning, Zeus took the child out of her body and put him in his own thigh for him to continue to grow.

FAMILY TREE

Son of Zeus and Semele

Husband to Ariane, with whom he had six children

With Aphrodite, he had Priapus

With Hera, Pasithea

WORSHIP

Dionysus, accompanied by a group of mad women, the maenads, the satyrs, and the panthers, is also the god of the theater, with plays performed in his honor.

DOLPHINS

Dionysus wanted to go to Naxos and asked some sailors to take him. But these pirates planned to sell him as a slave. Furious, the god transformed their oars into snakes and stopped the boat by making ivy grow on it. The pirates jumped into the water, where they changed into dolphins.

DRUNK AND CRAZY

Hera struck Dionysus with madness. He wandered around Egypt and Asia before coming to his senses. The king Lycurgus lifted the curse, but Dionysus then made him go mad: the king cut off his leg, thinking he was cutting the vine that Dionysus so loved.

21

CROWN

The god is often represented crowned with ivy or vines.

VASE

A vase holds the wine Dionysus drinks.

GOD
of the vine, of wine, and of drunkenness; protector of the theater

ROMAN NAME
Bacchus

THYRSUS

This rod, decorated with vines or ivy and topped by a pinecone, is the symbol of the god.

God of excess

Perseus

Acrisius, the king of Argos, had a beautiful daughter, Danae. An oracle prophesied that his daughter would have a son who'd kill him. Acrisius locked Danae in an underground room (or a bronze tower, in some tellings). But Zeus turned into a shower of gold and got in. From their union, Perseus was born. Thrown out of the city, Danae and Perseus drifted on the seas in a wooden box and ended up with Polydektes, the king of the island of Serifos. He asked Perseus to bring him the head of Medusa, a terrifying monster.

LOVERS

Having killed Medusa, Perseus saw a young girl sacrificed to a sea monster. He petrified the monster with Medusa's head and married the girl, Andromeda.

HUMANS

Hades's helmet made Perseus invisible. Thanks to Athena's shield, the hero saw the reflection of Medusa, thus glimpsing her without looking at her directly.

FAMILY TREE

Son of Zeus and Danae

Husband to Andromeda

Father of Perses, Electryon, Alcaeus, Sthenelus, Mestor, and Heleios

Ancestor of Heracles

THE GORGONS

There are three. Only Medusa is mortal. Their throats are covered with scales, they have boar tusks, and snakes for hair. If anyone trying to fight them meets the Gorgons' gaze, they are turned to stone.

THE PREDICTION

Perseus wanted to see his grandfather, but he kept escaping and left to take part in funeral games. Alas, the discus that Perseus threw in the course of the games hit Acrisius, who died from his wounds. You can't escape destiny!

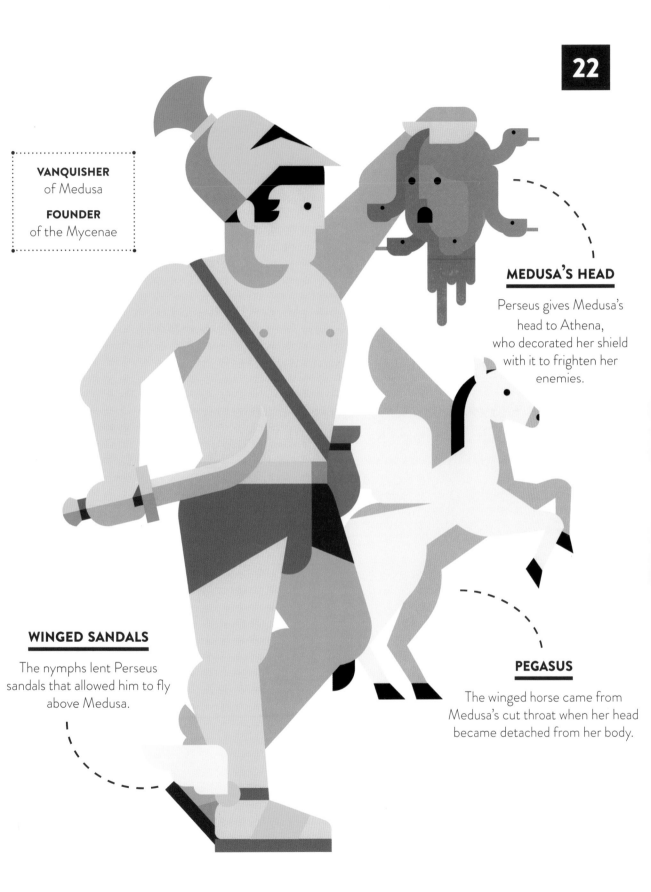

22

VANQUISHER
of Medusa

FOUNDER
of the Mycenae

MEDUSA'S HEAD

Perseus gives Medusa's head to Athena, who decorated her shield with it to frighten her enemies.

WINGED SANDALS

The nymphs lent Perseus sandals that allowed him to fly above Medusa.

PEGASUS

The winged horse came from Medusa's cut throat when her head became detached from her body.

The brave demi-god

Sisyphus

Sisyphus told Asopus that he had seen Zeus, king of the gods, kidnap Aegina, his daughter. To punish Sisyphus, Zeus sent him to the underworld. But things didn't go according to plan: Sisyphus imprisoned Thanatos, the spirit of death, and nobody else on earth died. Zeus intervened, and Sisyphus had to return to the underworld. But Sisyphus's trick managed to convince Hades and Persephone to let him go back to earth, where he could live a long life. After he had died, he was truly punished...

DEATH

Sisyphus had to roll a rock to the top of a hill in Tartarus. Each time he was on the point of succeeding, he gave way to the weight of the rock, which would then roll down the hill.

FAMILY TREE

Son of Aeolus and Enarete

Husband of a Pleiad, Merope, who he had four sons with: Almus, Glaucus, Ornytion, and Thersander

In a secret affair with Anticlea, who was promised to Laertes, he had a son, the cunning Odysseus

HUMANS

The expression "Sisyphean task" refers to a job without end, that has no chance of ever being completed, as it continuously has to be redone.

TWO ROBBERS MEET

Sisyphus noticed that his beasts were disappearing. To find the guilty party, he wrote his name under the animal's hoof. Thus he tricked Autolycus, who was about to transform his spoils. In revenge, Sisyphus got together with Anticlea, the daughter of the robber, who was supposed to get married the following day. From this union, Odysseus was born.

A CUNNING SON

Sisyphus is the father of the cunning Odysseus, the Trojan War hero whose adventures are described by Homer in the *Odyssey*. But where the father's intelligence is used for ill, the son's makes him a true hero.

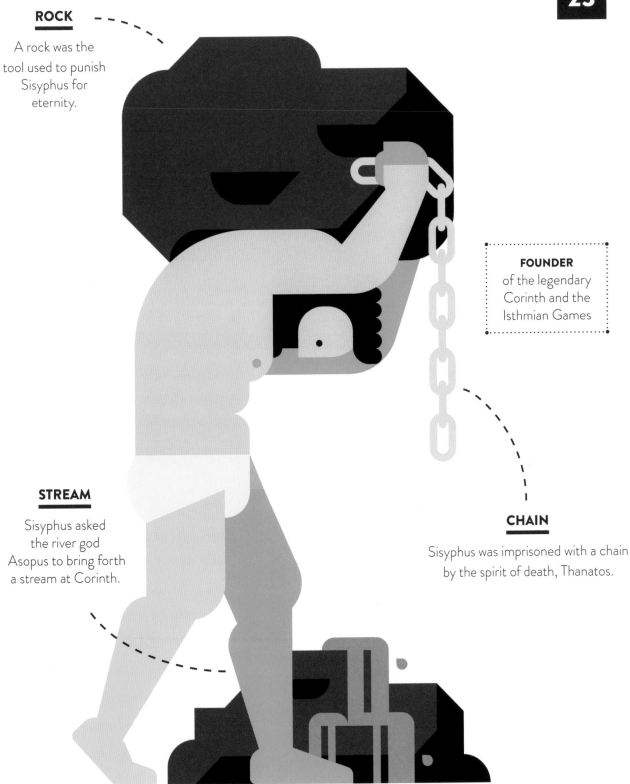

23

ROCK

A rock was the tool used to punish Sisyphus for eternity.

FOUNDER
of the legendary Corinth and the Isthmian Games

STREAM

Sisyphus asked the river god Asopus to bring forth a stream at Corinth.

CHAIN

Sisyphus was imprisoned with a chain by the spirit of death, Thanatos.

The man who defies the gods

HUMANS

Despite all his efforts to remain a free man, Oedipus couldn't escape his destiny, sealed by the gods before his birth.

Oedipus

CONFLICT

At a crossroads, Oedipus found himself face-to-face with an older traveler, who refused to let Oedipus pass. The young man was furious and killed him without suspecting that this man was, in fact, his father.

An oracle made a prophecy to Laius that "if you have a son, he will kill you and marry his mother." At Oedipus's birth, his father abandoned him. The baby was saved by shepherds working for Polybus, king of Corinth. The king was without an heir and adopted the infant. As an adult, Oedipus learned of the prophecy. Thinking it was about his adoptive parents, he fled Corinth. On his travels, he killed a man. Then he rid Thebes, his home country, of the sphinx and, as a reward, was offered the queen's hand in marriage.

FAMILY TREE

Son of Laius and Jocasta, rulers of Thebes

Husband to his own mother, Jocasta

Father to two boys, Eteocles and Polynices, and to two girls, Antigone and Ismene

THE RIDDLE OF THE SPHINX

The sphinx forbade access to Thebes to anyone who couldn't answer his riddle: "Who walks on four legs in the morning, on two legs at midday, and on three in the evening?" Oedipus replied, "It is a human who is a baby, then an adult and then walks with a stick." As a reward, the Thebans offered him their queen's hand in marriage. But the queen was actually his own mother.

THE PLAGUE

One day, a plague fell on Thebes. The Pythia declared that the illness would stop once Laius's murderer had been punished. Oedipus went to visit the seer Tiresias to attempt to discover the truth, never imagining that he himself was to blame.

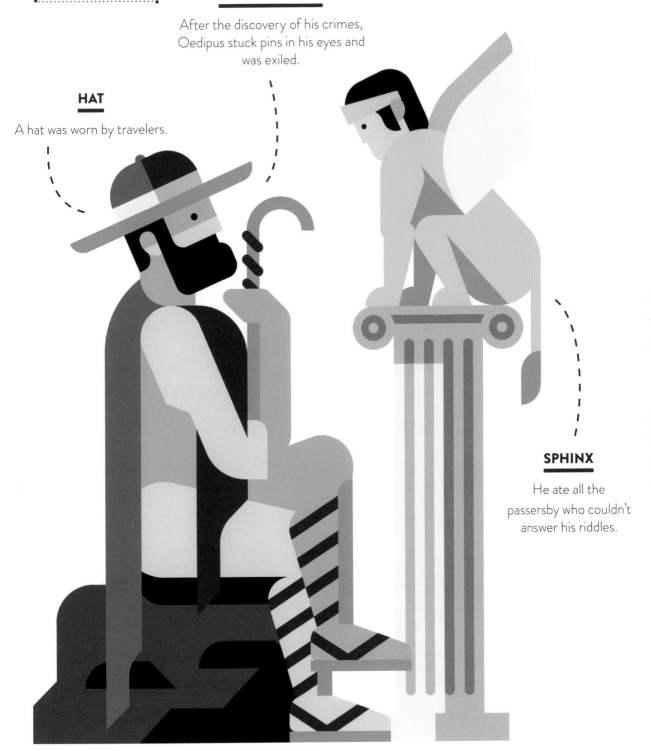

24

KING
of Thebes

WALKING STICK

After the discovery of his crimes,
Oedipus stuck pins in his eyes and
was exiled.

HAT

A hat was worn by travelers.

SPHINX

He ate all the
passersby who couldn't
answer his riddles.

A tragic destiny

Antigone

Antigone is the daughter of Oedipus and Jocasta. Oedipus was Jocasta's son, and he married her, not realizing she was his mother, as he had been abandoned at birth. When Oedipus found out the truth, he blinded himself as a punishment and exiled himself from the town; Jocasta killed herself. Antigone decided to leave with her father. When he died, she returned to Thebes, where a war for power was taking place. There, she again fulfilled her familial duties.

RETURN TO THEBES

Ismene joined Antigone and their father at Colonus. The sisters returned to Thebes, where war was raging. Eteocles fought in the Theban army, and his brother, Polynices, in the Argive army, which was attacking the city. The two brothers killed each other.

CONFLICT

Creon ordered Antigone to be buried alive for having attempted to bury and mourn her brother.

DEATH

Creon forbade Polynices from being buried, as he had fought against his country. Antigone felt that it was her duty to bury her brother. A bit of earth thrown on the body was enough.

BLOODBATH

The tragedy of Oedipus continued after his death. His daughter Antigone killed herself. Upon discovering her, Haemon, her fiancé, who was also Creon's son, committed suicide over her lifeless body. Creon's wife, Eurydice, also died. Of Oedipus's children, three died young: Antigone, Polynices, and Eteocles. Only Ismene survived.

FAMILY TREE

Daughter of Oedipus and Jocasta

Creon's niece

Sister to Eteocles, Polynices, and Ismene

25

PRINCESS
of Thebes

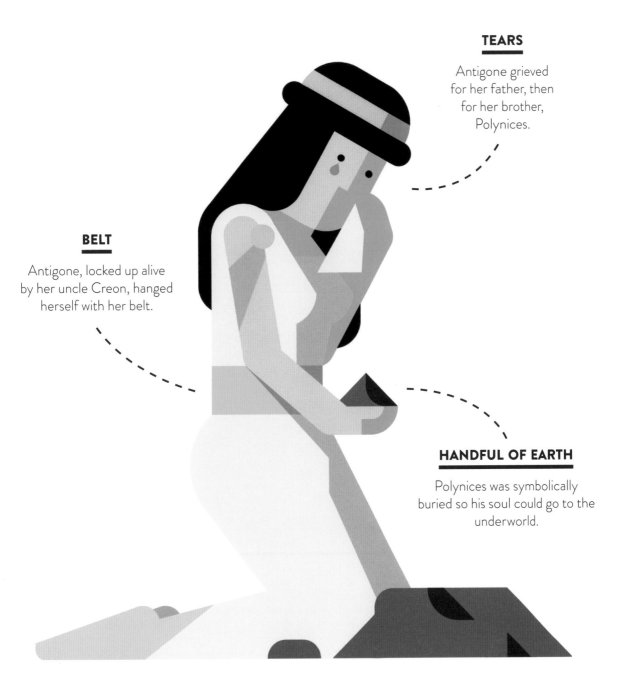

TEARS

Antigone grieved
for her father, then
for her brother,
Polynices.

BELT

Antigone, locked up alive
by her uncle Creon, hanged
herself with her belt.

HANDFUL OF EARTH

Polynices was symbolically
buried so his soul could go to the
underworld.

Filial love

Heracles

Heracles and his half brother were sleeping in their crib. Hera put two snakes into the room to kill them, but Heracles woke up and suffocated them.

Heracles had to endure Hera's hatred from birth because he was the son of Zeus and a mortal. He had twelve tasks to complete: killing the lion at Nemea, getting rid of the Hydra of Lerna, neutralizing the bull of Erymanthus, capturing the Ceryneian deer, scaring the birds of lake Stymphalus, cleaning the stables at Augea, taming the bull of Crete, taking Diomedes's mares, stealing the Amazon queen's belt, capturing the cattle of Geryon, taking apples from the garden of the Hesperides, and mastering Cerberus.

LINKED TO HERA

For his whole life, this hero was the goddess Hera's plaything. She wanted him to fail, but he emerged victorious from the most difficult tests. However, when she made him go mad and kill his own children, Heracles was not able to resist her.

DEED

During the course of one of his voyages, Heracles saw Prometheus attached to a rock. With a single arrow, he killed the eagle that each day ate the liver of poor Prometheus.

IMMORTAL?

Hermes put Heracles near sleeping Hera. The baby breastfed from the goddess, which rendered him immortal. Years later, he was poisoned by Deianira. He suffered so much that he burned himself on a log. Zeus took him to Olympus.

FAMILY TREE

Son of Zeus and Alcmene

Half brother of Iphicles

Husband to Megara, then Deianira

Father to numerous children

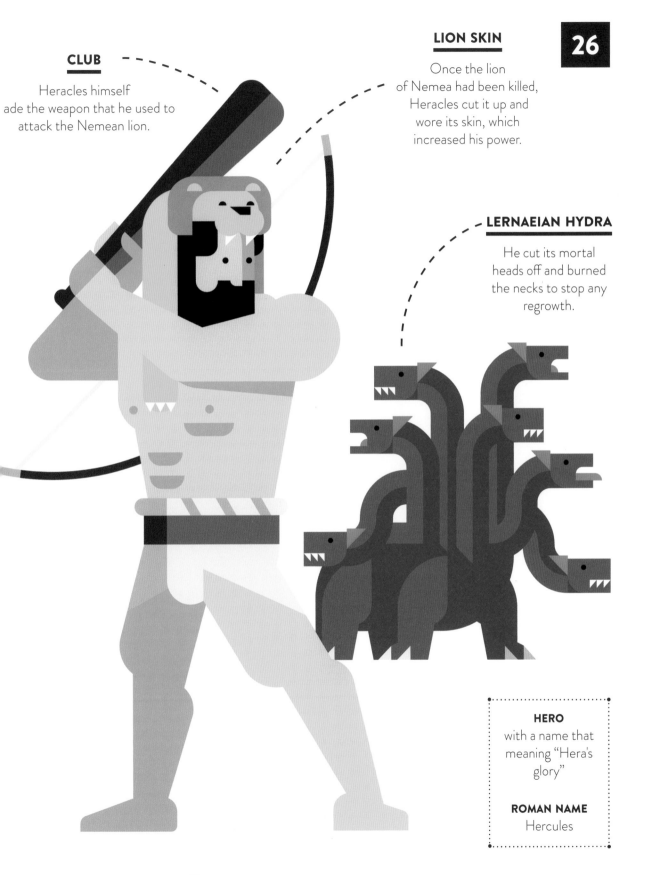

26

CLUB

Heracles himself
ade the weapon that he used to
attack the Nemean lion.

LION SKIN

Once the lion
of Nemea had been killed,
Heracles cut it up and
wore its skin, which
increased his power.

LERNAEIAN HYDRA

He cut its mortal
heads off and burned
the necks to stop any
regrowth.

HERO
with a name that
meaning "Hera's
glory"

ROMAN NAME
Hercules

A courageous hero

DEATH

When Orpheus died, his lyre was transformed into a constellation It is said his soul sings for the dead who wander the Elysian Fields.

Orpheus

Orpheus sings and plays the lyre so beautifully that no one can resist his music. He took part in the expedition of Jason and the Argonauts, taming the sirens trying to attract the sailors to eat them. He even made an impression on Hades and Persephone: the gods of the underworld, touched by his songs and his love for his wife, Eurydice, allowed him to take her back to earth—on the condition that he didn't turn around on the way out. At the last moment, he checked that she was behind him, and she died for a second time.

WORSHIP

Rituals and poems linked to the mysteries of death have been written in memory of Orpheus. They were no doubt said during secret ceremonies.

EURYDICE

Orpheus's wife, Eurydice, ran barefoot through the countryside to escape the attentions of Aristaeus. She died after a snake bit her on the foot. Orpheus was inconsolable and decided to attempt the impossible and went to look for his love in the underworld.

THE MYSTERIES OF ORPHEUS

According to one myth, when he returned to the underworld, Orpheus created secret groups that did not admit women. One night, some women took the weapons that the faithful had left at the door of the temple, went in, and killed them.

FAMILY TREE

Son of Oeagrus, the king of Thace, and the muse of poetry, Calliope

Husband to Eurydice

27

LYRE

Orpheus
is believed to have
invented the lyre.

HERO
of the Argonaut
expedition

BEAST

All creatures
e charmed by Orpheus's music.

SNAKE

Eurydice died
from a snake bite.
Orpheus was grief-stricken.

The greatest musician

Jason

Jason is the son of Aeson, king of Iolcos, a city in Thessaly. When Aeson was removed from power by his half brother Pelias, Jason was given to Chiron, the centaur, who hid him and taught him everything he knew. The new king, Pelias, was afraid of one thing: an oracle had told him to beware of a man wearing only one sandal. Years later, Jason came back to Iolcos—wearing only one sandal. Pelias challenged him to bring back a precious object, guarded night and day by a dragon: the Golden Fleece.

DEED

To go and get the Golden Fleece, Jason needed a boat with fifty rowers. He took the *Argo*, a magic ship that had been built by the carpenter Argos with Athena's help.

FAMILY TREE

Son of Aeson

With Hypsipyle, he had twins, Euneus and Nebrophon

With Medea, he had a son, Medus. According to some versions of the story, they also had a daughter, Eriopis, and two other boys, Pheres and Mermeros.

Jason then married Creusa

DEATH

To protect their young son who had been given to Chiron, Aeson and his wife organized a fake funeral.

THE ARGONAUTS

Jason was well supported for this perilous sea journey. Around fifty heroes went with him to distant Colchis. Some were sons of Zeus; the others, children of Hermes and Poseidon. Orpheus set the pace for the rowers and kept the Sirens at bay with his wonderful singing. Heracles also went on the trip.

THE GOLDEN FLEECE

How could they get the precious Fleece from King Aeëtes? Medea, the king's daughter, fell madly in love with Jason at first sight. And thanks to the help of this beautiful sorceress, the hero managed to get ahold of the trophy.

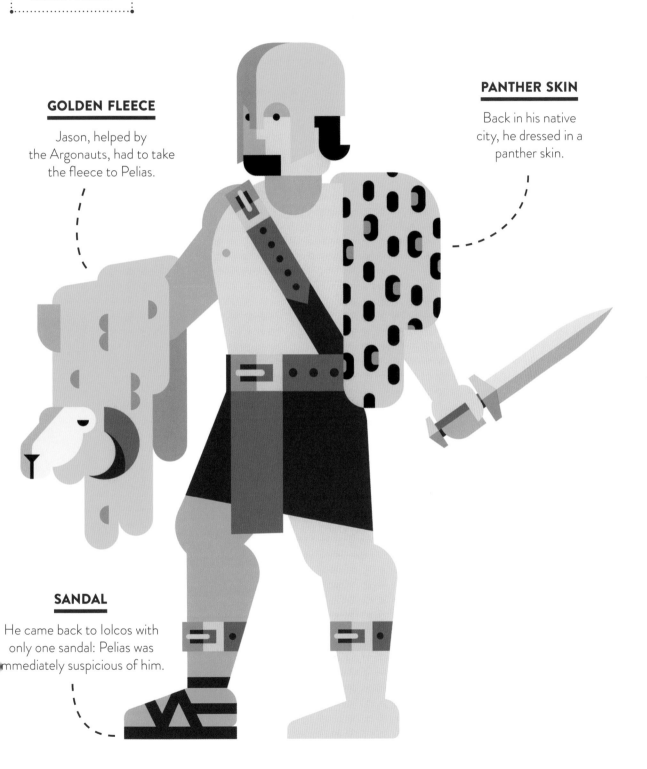

28

HERO
that captured the
Golden Fleece

GOLDEN FLEECE

Jason, helped by
the Argonauts, had to take
the fleece to Pelias.

PANTHER SKIN

Back in his native
city, he dressed in a
panther skin.

SANDAL

He came back to Iolcos with
only one sandal: Pelias was
immediately suspicious of him.

The captain of the Argonauts

Medea

When the Argonauts reached the lands of King Aeëtes, his daughter, the princess Medea, only had eyes for the handsome Jason. She decided to help him acquire the Golden Fleece, on one condition: he would take her back to Greece with him when the task was accomplished. Jason agreed. Thanks to Medea, Jason was victorious: she gave him a balm that protected him against the fire breathed by Hephaestus's bulls, and she showed him how to escape from the armies that came out of the ground.

THE TESTS

Aeëtes ordered Jason to put two bulls in a yoke. Then Jason had to make the bulls plow a field and sow dragon's teeth that would grow into soldiers. He threw a stone into their midst, and they killed each other.

FAMILY TREE

The daughter of the king Aeëtes

Had two sons with Jason, Pheres and Mermeros

In some versions of the myth, she has a daughter, Eriopis, and another son, Medus, with Jason

THE ESCAPE

Aeëtes, a sore loser, refused to hand over the Golden Fleece. Jason had to take it by force, but it was guarded by a terrible dragon. Medea used her magic to make it go to sleep. Jason took the fleece and escaped by boat with his companions and the princess.

CONFLICT

Medea took her younger brother Absyrtus as a hostage. To put distance between the fleet and her father, she killed her brother, cut him into pieces, and threw his body into the sea.

DESCENDANTS

Later, Jason abandoned Medea to marry Creusa, princess of Corinth. Medea poisoned her rival and killed the children that she herself had had with Jason.

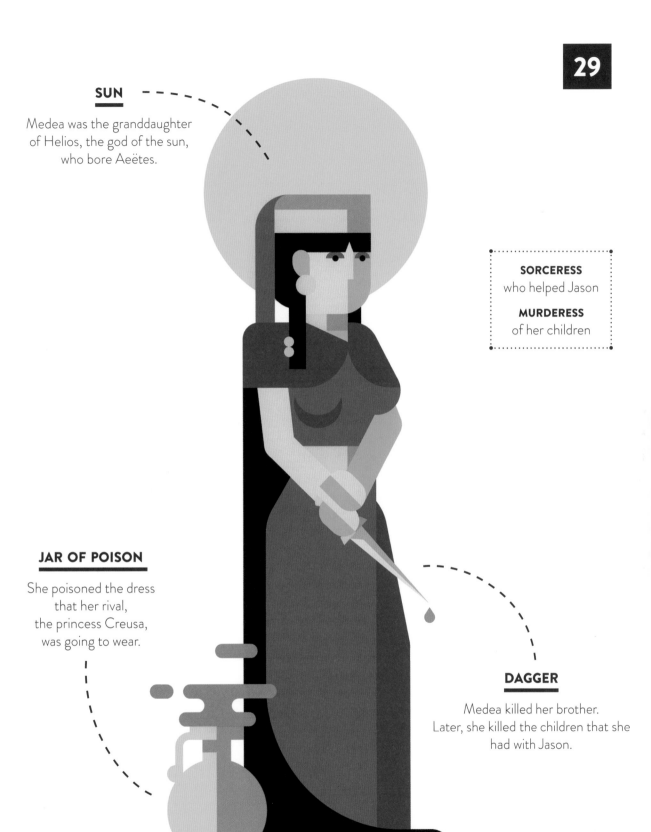

29

SUN

Medea was the granddaughter of Helios, the god of the sun, who bore Aeëtes.

SORCERESS
who helped Jason

MURDERESS
of her children

JAR OF POISON

She poisoned the dress that her rival, the princess Creusa, was going to wear.

DAGGER

Medea killed her brother. Later, she killed the children that she had with Jason.

A princess sorceress

Minotaur

Zeus gave a white bull to Minos, the king of Crete, for him to sacrifice it to Poseidon. But Minos found the bull so beautiful that he decided to keep it for himself. Divine punishment soon manifested itself: Pasiphae, Minos's wife, gave birth to a son with the head of a bull. The child was named Asterius, but everybody called it the Minotaur. Minos asked Daedalus the architect to make him a maze: a palace with rooms and corridors so complex that the child-monster could never escape.

DAEDALUS AND ICARUS

Minos imprisoned Daedalus and Icarus in the Labyrinth so they couldn't reveal his plans. Daedalus built wings out of wax and feathers, and escaped into the air with his son. But Icarus, drawn to the sun, flew too high. The wax melted and he fell.

HUMANS

Asterius, an innocent victim, is the person Poseidon punished for Minos's lack of respect. In the Labyrinth, he becomes cruel and asks to eat young Athenians.

MINOS'S PALACE

It's thought that the Labyrinth is the mythical image of the vast and complex palace where Minos ruled Crete, a Greek island in the Mediterranean. This island was a stopping point for sailors transporting goods between Egypt and continental Greece.

FAMILY TREE

Son of a bull, given by Zeus and the queen of Crete, Pasiphae

Half brother to Ariadne and Phaedra

30

MONSTER
with a human body and the head of a bull

LABYRINTH
It was in this palace, where it was impossible to find your way out, that Minos left him.

HEAD OF A BULL
This Cretian prince was born as a monster because Poseidon visited upon him the insult of his father, Minos.

DAGGER
A dagger was the weapon the Athenian hero, Theseus, fatally wounded him with.

The monster of the Labyrinth

Theseus

Aegeus, king of Athens, had no son to succeed him. He went to consult the oracle at Delphi, who said, "Do not loosen the bulging mouth of the wine skin until you have reached the height of Athens, lest you die of grief." On the way home, Aegeus stopped at Troezen. The city's king got him drunk, opened the wine skin, and put him in bed with his daughter, Aethra. Aegeus said to Aethra, "If you have a son, don't send him to Athens until he is 16. By these sandals and this sword that I will hide under this rock, I will know him."

DANGEROUS JOURNEY

At 16, armed with the sword and sandals left by his father, Aegeus, the boy decided to join him. On the way, he put an end to the bandits Sinis and Pertes. In Athens, he was about to be poisoned by Medea, the queen, but just in time, his father recognized him.

FAMILY TREE

Son of Aegeus, king of Athens, and Aethra, daughter of the king of Troezen

His affair with the Amazonian Antiope led to a son, Hippolytus

AGAINST THE MINOTAUR

Every nine years, Crete demanded seven girls and seven boys from Athens to feed to the Minotaur. Theseus managed to slip in with them to kill the monster. Aegeus asked him to raise white sails on his boat on the way home to show that he was alive.

LOVERS

Ariadne, the Minotaur's half sister, fell in love with Theseus. Without her help, the Athenian prince could not have destroyed the monster.

DEATH

Theseus forgot to raise white sails. Seeing black ones, Aegeus believed his son to be dead. Grief-stricken, he threw himself into the sea that has borne his name ever since.

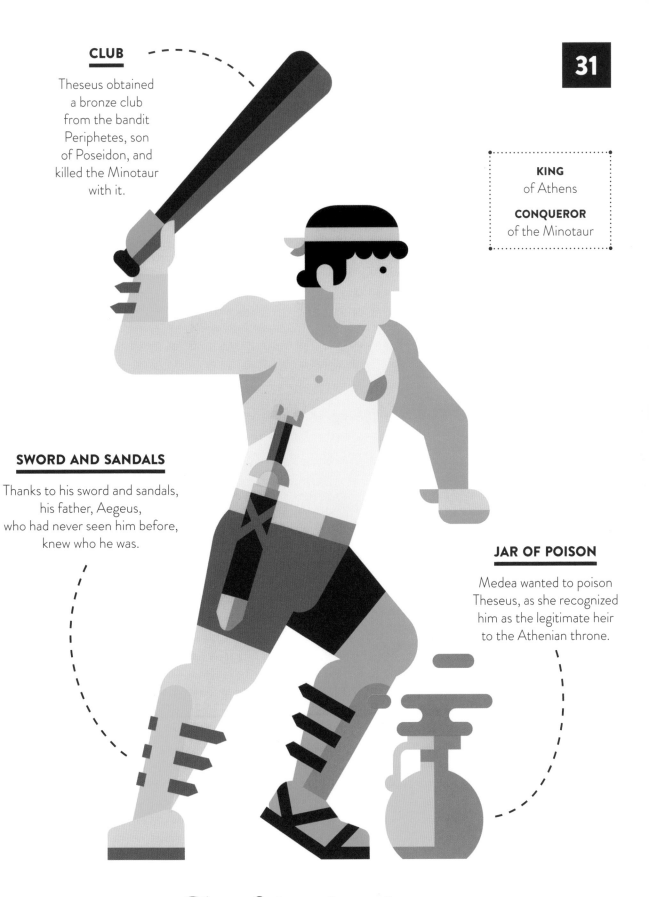

31

CLUB

Theseus obtained a bronze club from the bandit Periphetes, son of Poseidon, and killed the Minotaur with it.

KING
of Athens
CONQUEROR
of the Minotaur

SWORD AND SANDALS

Thanks to his sword and sandals, his father, Aegeus, who had never seen him before, knew who he was.

JAR OF POISON

Medea wanted to poison Theseus, as she recognized him as the legitimate heir to the Athenian throne.

The Athenian hero

Ariadne

A Cretian princess, Ariadne, the daughter of Minos, saw her half brother Asterius get shut in the Labyrinth. From then on known as the Minotaur, the prince became a solitary and bloodthirsty being. Every nine years, he ate fourteen young Athenians, chosen and delivered to him by King Minos. When Ariadne saw Theseus arriving among these victims, she fell madly in love with him. She gave him the means to kill the Minotaur in exchange for a promise: afterward, he had to take her with him.

DEED

Ariadne gave a ball of wool to Theseus. He unwound it as he went around the Labyrinth and then followed it back again to get out of the complex architecture.

CONFLICT

Ariadne also gave Theseus a dagger so that he could kill the monster. The young Athenians had arrived without weapons.

THE ESCAPE

After having killed the Minotaur, Theseus left with his companions. Faithful to his promise, he took Ariadne. They stopped at the island of Naxos, while beautiful Ariadne slept peacefully next to the man she loved. When she awoke, she was alone: Theseus had abandoned her!

ARIADNE ON NAXOS

According to some of the stories, Dionysus arrived on Naxos on his chariot drawn by panthers. He found Ariadne so beautiful that he married her and took her to Olympus. In other versions of the story, Dionysus orders Artemis to kill Ariadne.

FAMILY TREE

Daughter of Minos and Pasiphae

Half sister of the Minotaur and sister to Phaedra

Wife of Dionysus, with whom she had children: Keramos, Thoas, Oenopion, Peparethos, and Staphylos

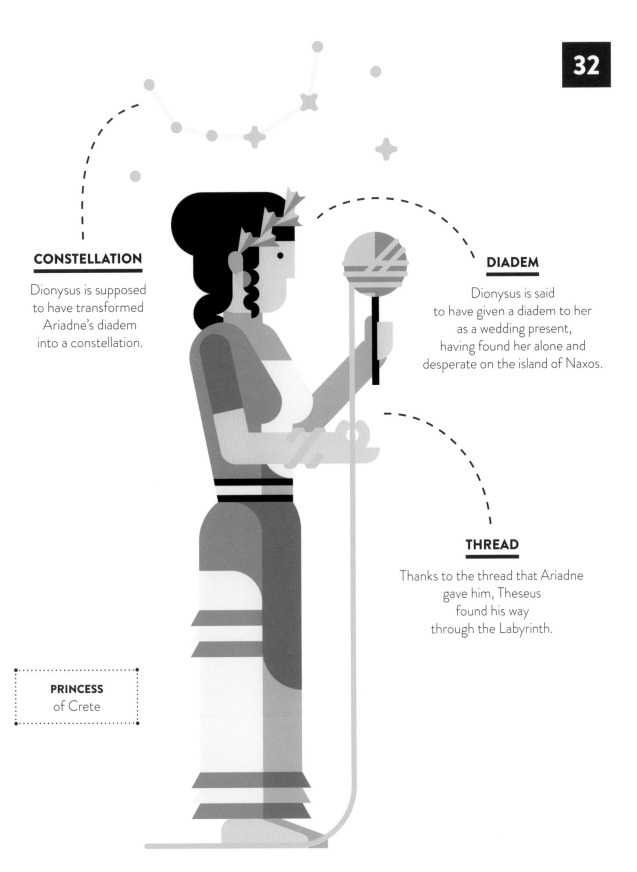

32

CONSTELLATION

Dionysus is supposed to have transformed Ariadne's diadem into a constellation.

DIADEM

Dionysus is said to have given a diadem to her as a wedding present, having found her alone and desperate on the island of Naxos.

THREAD

Thanks to the thread that Ariadne gave him, Theseus found his way through the Labyrinth.

PRINCESS
of Crete

The abandoned lover

Phaedra

The Cretian Deucalion was friends with Theseus, who became king of Athens. Although Theseus had abandoned one of Deucalion's sisters, Ariadne, Deucalion decided to give him his other sister, Phaedra, in marriage. To marry this young woman, Theseus had to renounce Antiope the Amazon, by whom he had a son named Hippolytus. When Phaedra arrived at the Athenian court, she was blown away by the beauty of the boy she had to consider her son. This love, brought about by Aphrodite, ruined her, and the young man.

ANTIOPE

Antiope was rejected by Theseus, who wanted to marry Phaedra. She couldn't bear the insult. She got together with her sisters, the Amazons, and together they attacked Athens on the day of the king's wedding. Antiope died during the attack.

FAMILY TREE

Daughter of Minos and Pasiphae

Sister to Ariadne and half sister of the Minotaur

Wife of Theseus

Mother to Acamas and Demophon

FORBIDDEN LOVE

Phaedra declared her love to Hippolytus, but he did not feel the same way. Desperate, Phaedra tore her clothes, wrote a letter in which she accused Hippolytus of having wanted to seduce her, and then hanged herself.

DEATH

Theseus had chased away Antiope, then lost Phaedra, who, from beyond the grave, persuaded him to kill his own son, Hippolytus. The tragedy was complete.

CONFLICT

Theseus, believing himself to be betrayed, asked Poseidon to kill his son. The god made a monster that scared Hippolytus's horses. The prince was crushed to death.

33

PRINCESS
of Crete

QUEEN
of Athens

ROPE

Humiliated
and worried that her
actions might
be discovered
by Theseus, Phaedra
ended her life.

SEA MONSTER

He caused the death of
Hippolytus,
Phaedra's stepson.

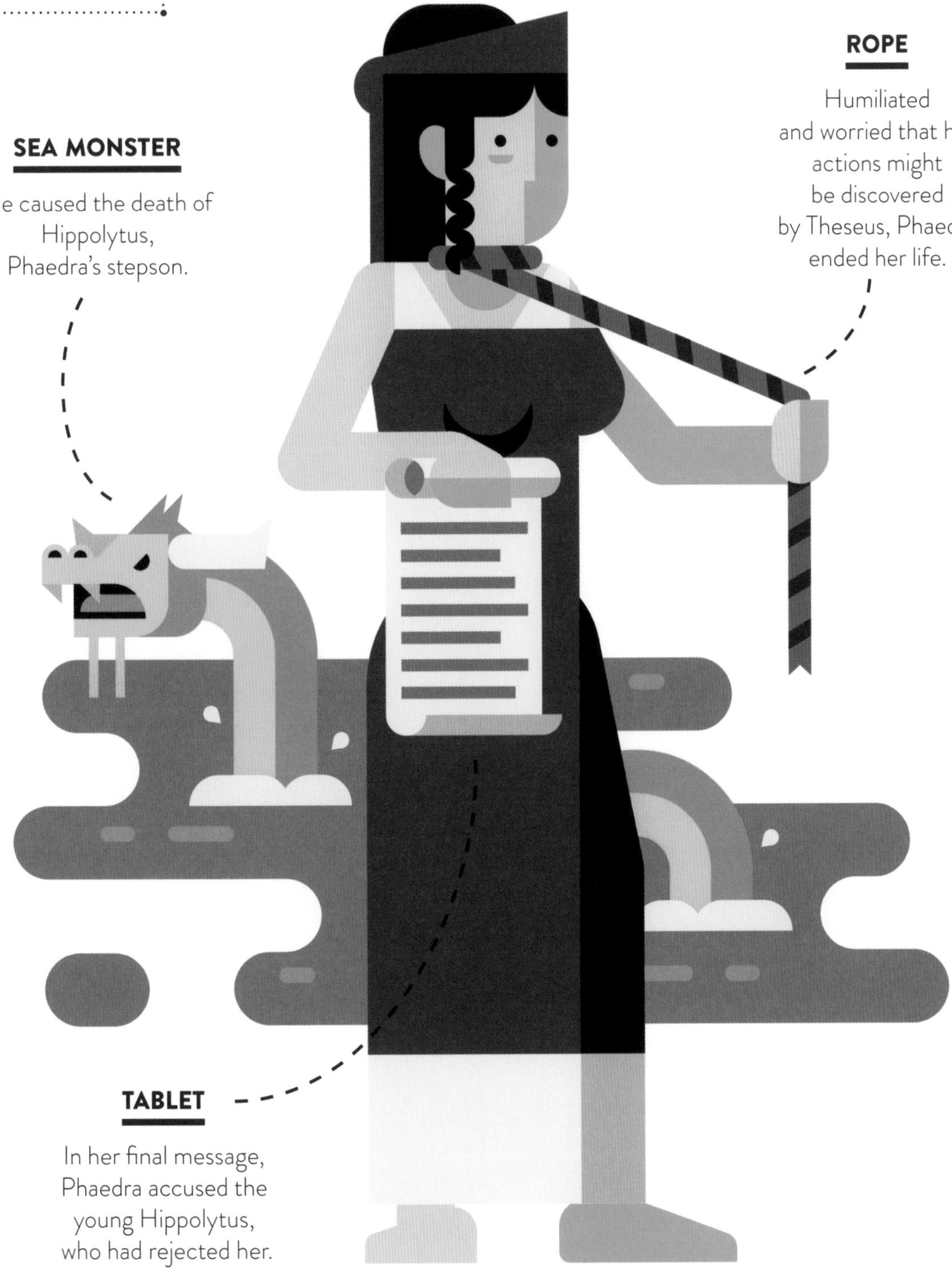

TABLET

In her final message,
Phaedra accused the
young Hippolytus,
who had rejected her.

A tragic heroine

Tantalus

Tantalus reigned on Mount Sipylus, in Lydia. The gods liked him so much that they invited him to their banquets. But one day, Tantalus refused to give Hermes back a golden dog that had been brought up with Zeus. Hermes found the animal, and Tantalus was shut up for a long time under Mount Sipylus. Later, the gods came to earth to dine at the king's table. Tantalus had killed his son Pelops and served him up to the gods, possibly in order to test their ability to know everything. But his pride cost him dearly.

HUMANS

The gods noticed there was something strange about the food they were being served. They realized that it was human flesh. Worse, it was their host's child!

DEATH

The sacrilege that Tantalus had committed could only be punished by death. But that was not enough. The gods decided that Tantalus would suffer eternal torture.

HUNGER AND THIRST

Tantalus was put in water up to his throat, while above his head, a tree hung with fruit. He was hungry and thirsty, but each time he tried to drink the water, it receded, and when he tried to eat the fruit, a gust of wind would blow the branch out of reach.

ETYMOLOGY

The torture invented by the gods to punish his barbaric act gives us our word "to tantalize," which is to excite a hope and then disappoint it.

FAMILY TREE

Son of Zeus and Plouto

Husband to the Pleiad Dione, daughter of Atlas; or possibly Euryanassa

Father to Pelops and Niobe

34

FRUIT TREE

The fruit on the tree was forever inaccessible to the tortured Tantalus.

KING
of Lydia
(in Asia Minor)

CAULDRON

Tantalus cooked the flesh of his son in a cauldron before serving it to the gods.

IN WATER

Up to his neck in water, Tantalus was tormented by thirst.

The tortured king

CONFLICT

The myth says that it was in order to free Helen that the Greeks, allied with Menelaus, laid siege to Troy for ten years.

Helen

Helen was so beautiful that all the Greek kings wanted to marry her. Embarrassed, her father, Tyndareus, promised all suitors that he would accept whatever choice Helen made and would help her if she were ever in danger. Helen chose Menelaus, the king of the city of Sparta. But she was soon kidnapped by Paris as his reward for having elected Aphrodite as the most beautiful goddess. The Greeks united right away to help Menelaus find his wife. The Trojan War was declared.

LOVERS

Paris was rich and seductive. Helen ran off with him to Troy, abandoning her husband and daughter. Some people say the gods intervened.

HELEN AND THE TROJANS

Priam, the king of Troy, liked Helen. His oldest son, Hector, agreed with him, and his youngest son, Paris, was in love with her. The rest of the Trojans, on the other hand, didn't like her, as they held her responsible for the war.

CHOSEN

When the goddess Aphrodite was elected the most beautiful of the goddesses by Paris, she gave him in return the most beautiful of mortals, Helen. Legend has it that Aphrodite made Paris look like Menelaus to allow him to take her.

FAMILY TREE

Daughter of Tyndareus, chief of Sparta (though possibly fathered by Zeus), and Leda

Wife of Menelaus

Mother to Hermione

Taken by Paris

35

BEAUTY

The immense beauty of Helen caused much misery.

QUEEN
of Sparta

REASON
for the war between the Greeks and Trojans

EGG

Helen is said to have been born in an egg, as Zeus had transformed himself into a swan to seduce Leda.

PROMISE

On the skin of a sacrificed horse, the suitors promised to help her husband if Helen was taken.

The most beautiful of mortals

Agamemnon

Agamemnon married Clytemnestra, Helen's sister, having killed her first husband and her newborn. With this double murder, the story of King Agamemnon is marked by tragedy. Once Helen had been taken by Paris, Agamemnon became the chief of the Greek expedition to Troy to bring her back. But he and Achilles, the Greek hero, didn't get along. When Agamemnon demanded that Achilles give him his slave, Briseis, the siege of Troy turned to catastrophe.

TWO SLAVES ...

During the battles against Troy, Achilles acquired Queen Briseis as a slave and they fell in love with each other. Agamemnon acquired Chryseis. But she was the daughter of Chryses, a priest of Apollo. The god would not put up with such an insult.

FAMILY TREE

Son of Atreus and Aerope

Brother to Menelaus

Husband to Clytemnestra

Father to Orestes, Electra, Iphigenia, and Chrysothemis

A MAD RAGE

Apollo sent a plague to punish Agamemnon. That left Agamemnon with no choice but to give Chryseis back. In exchange, he demanded that Achilles give him Briseis. Achilles obeyed but was so angry that he refused to fight.

CONFLICT

After the Trojan War, Agamemnon went back to Greece with the Trojan Cassandra. Clytemnestra killed him for having cheated on her and for having tried to sacrifice their daughter Iphigenia.

HUMANS

Zeus sent the king a dream to make him believe that the Greeks could defeat the Trojans, even without Achilles's help. But it wasn't true.

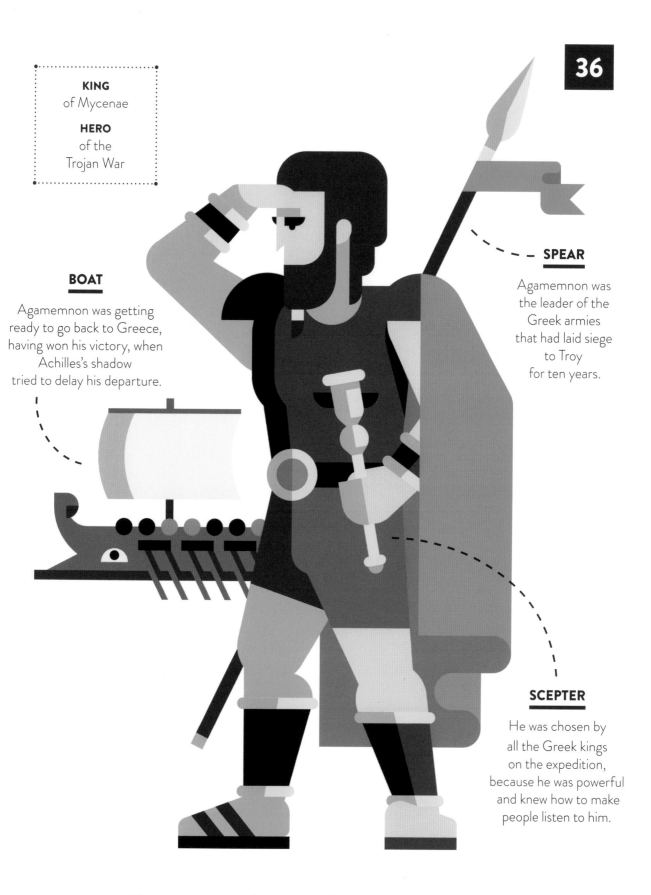

36

KING
of Mycenae

HERO
of the
Trojan War

SPEAR

Agamemnon was
the leader of the
Greek armies
that had laid siege
to Troy
for ten years.

BOAT

Agamemnon was getting
ready to go back to Greece,
having won his victory, when
Achilles's shadow
tried to delay his departure.

SCEPTER

He was chosen by
all the Greek kings
on the expedition,
because he was powerful
and knew how to make
people listen to him.

Leader of the Greek army

Iphigenia

Agamemnon was head of the Greek flotilla of around a hundred ships that were going to Troy to free Helen. But before leaving, he killed a deer sacred to Artemis, so the furious goddess summoned wild winds and the boats couldn't leave the harbor at Aulis. According to Calchas the seer, Artemis would only calm down if Agamemnon sacrificed his own daughter, Iphigenia. The king submitted to her demands and got the princess to come from Mycenae on the pretext that he wanted to marry her to Achilles.

THE SACRIFICE

As soon as the young girl arrived at Aulis, the seer, Calchas, put her on an altar dedicated to Artemis. He was about to kill her as an offering to the goddess. At the last minute, Artemis made a deer appear, which was sacrificed in Iphigenia's place.

WORSHIP

Artemis led Iphigenia to Tauris and made her a priestess. The young girl was made to sacrifice foreigners who were shipwrecked there.

THE ESCAPE

Orestes killed his mother to avenge his father, but this murder made him mad. According to the oracle, the only hope he had of coming to his senses was to find the statue of Artemis, fallen from heaven, so he left for Tauris. Iphigenia recognized her brother and escaped with him.

FAMILY TREE

Daughter of Agamemnon and Clytemnestra

Sister of Chrysothemis, Electra, and Orestes

37

PRIESTESS
of Artemis

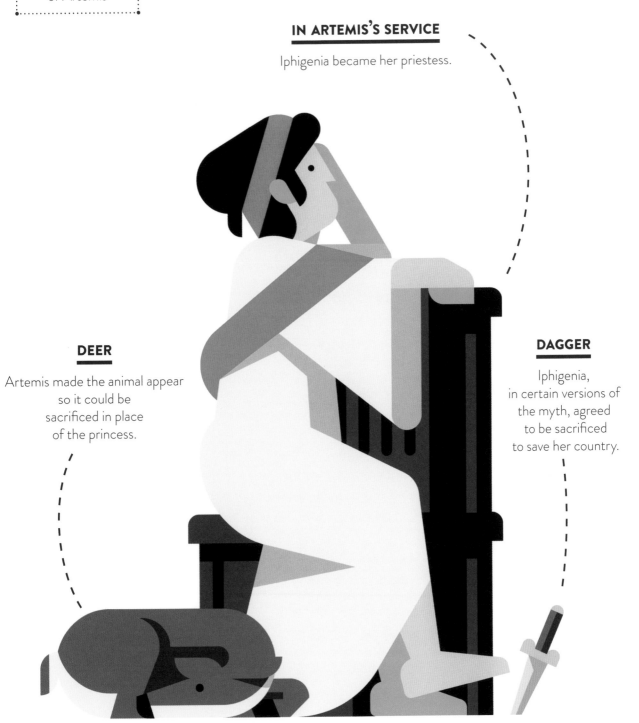

IN ARTEMIS'S SERVICE

Iphigenia became her priestess.

DEER

Artemis made the animal appear
so it could be
sacrificed in place
of the princess.

DAGGER

Iphigenia,
in certain versions of
the myth, agreed
to be sacrificed
to save her country.

A sacrificed princess

Electra

Clytemnestra, helped by her lover, Aegisthus, killed her husband, King Agamemnon. Electra, Clytemnestra and Agamemnon's daughter, was also threatened, but her mother intervened. Electra saved her brother, Orestes, who was brought up out of the country with Pylades, their cousin. At Mycenae, Electra lived under Aegisthus's watch: he feared she'd have a son who'd seek vengeance. When Orestes came back to Mycenae as an adult, he rediscovered his sister. Together, they killed their mother and the usurper Aegisthus.

CONFLICT

Electra announced to the court that her brother, Orestes, had died. Taking advantage of the commotion brought about by this false news, the brother and sister committed the murders.

FAMILY TREE

Daughter of Agamemnon and Clytemnestra

Sister to Chryosthemis, Iphigenia, and Orestes

Wife of Pylades

HUMANS

The Furies sent Orestes mad for having killed his mother. Electra protected her brother against these half women, half birds who embodied the gods' fury.

BROTHER AND SISTERS MEET UP

Orestes left for Tauris to look for Artemis's statue, which was supposed to cure his madness. At Mycenae, a rumor went around: the young man had been killed by his own sister, Iphigenia. Electra went to his aid and tried to blind Iphigenia to avenge Orestes but saw him just in time. The sisters and brother were finally reunited and escaped together to Greece.

THE RETURN

Orestes, Electra, and Iphigenia went back to Mycenae. Aletes, Aegisthus's son, had taken power. They killed him, and the throne finally returned to Agamemnon's descendants. Electra married Pylades, her cousin and Orestes's friend.

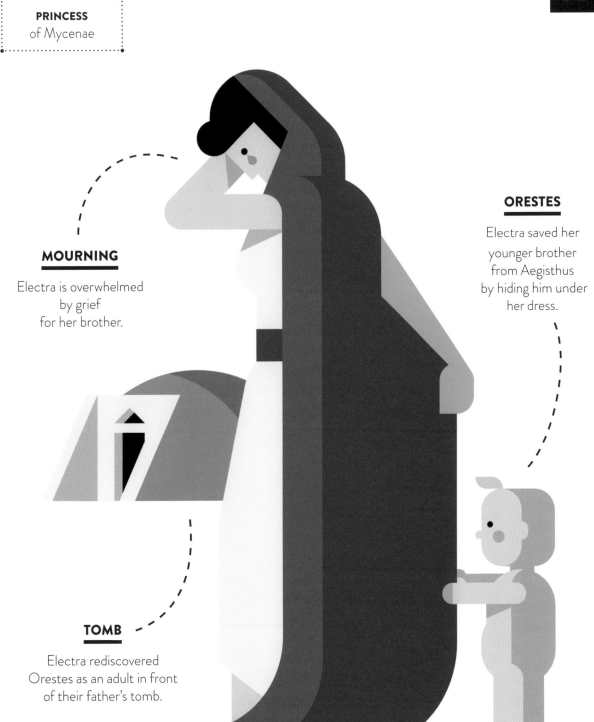

38

PRINCESS
of Mycenae

MOURNING

Electra is overwhelmed
by grief
for her brother.

ORESTES

Electra saved her
younger brother
from Aegisthus
by hiding him under
her dress.

TOMB

Electra rediscovered
Orestes as an adult in front
of their father's tomb.

A willing princess

Achilles

CONFLICT

Achilles's mother had told him he would fight the Trojans and that he would have a short life, but he preferred glory to a long and miserable existence.

Son of a mortal and of Thetis, the goddess of water, Achilles was practically invincible. Only his heel, which his mother held him by while dipping him in the river Styx to make him immortal, could be injured. Achilles was the biggest hero of the Trojan War. After nine years of seige, he got very angry when Agamemnon, another Greek leader, took his slave, Briseis, whom he loved. So he refused to fight. He only took up arms again after the death in battle of his dear friend Patroclus.

PATROCLUS'S DEATH

When Achilles stopped fighting, his friend Patroclus begged Achilles to lend him his armor so he could fight the Trojans in Achilles's place. Achilles agreed. During a terrible battle, Hector, a Trojan, killed Patroclus. Achilles arranged a big funeral for his friend.

DEATH

After having killed Hector, Achilles carried the body of the deceased on his chariot. The gods' anger ended up forcing the Greek warrior to accept a decent burial for his enemy.

AGAINST HECTOR

After the death of Patroclus, Achilles returned to fight with new armor. The gods prevented Achilles and Hector from fighting, until the point where the Fates decided that the time had come. Achilles then killed his friend's murderer.

FAMILY TREE

Son of Peleus, king of Myrmidons, and the nymph Thetis, goddess of water

Father to Neoptolemus

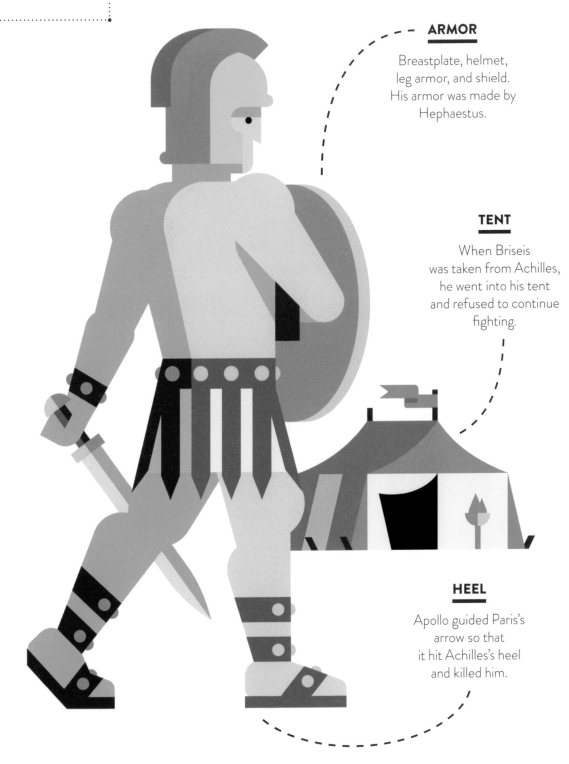

ARMOR

Breastplate, helmet, leg armor, and shield. His armor was made by Hephaestus.

TENT

When Briseis was taken from Achilles, he went into his tent and refused to continue fighting.

HEEL

Apollo guided Paris's arrow so that it hit Achilles's heel and killed him.

The hero of the *Iliad*

Odysseus

Odysseus was one of the Greek warriors who laid siege to Troy for ten years. He distinguished himself by his courage and even more so by his cunning intelligence. Once the war was over, won by the Greeks, Odysseus went back by sea to Ithaca, the island where he was king. But for ten years, various adventures, brought about by Poseidon's anger, delayed his return. When he finally arrived, he retook his throne and reunited with his wife, Penelope, who had waited for him all that time.

DEED

On their return voyage, Odysseus's companions were well looked after by the Lotophagi, who gave them delicious fruit. They didn't want to leave!

CONFLICT

Odysseus built a wooden horse in which he and other warriors hid. He made the Trojans believe that it was a gift from the Greeks, who were abandoning the siege.

FAMILY TREE

Son of Laertes (or Sisyphus) and Anticlea

Husband to Penelope

Father to Telemachus

"NOBODY"

Odysseus and his companions were trapped by the Cyclops Polyphemus. Odysseus made him believe that his name was "Nobody." He managed to escape by blinding the monster. When Polyphemus warned his brothers he had been blinded by Nobody, they mocked him.

PENELOPE

For twenty years, Penelope waited for her husband to return. She said that she would not remarry until she had woven Laertes's shroud. However at night, she undid what she had done in the day. When Odysseus finally returned, he killed his wife's eight hundred suitors.

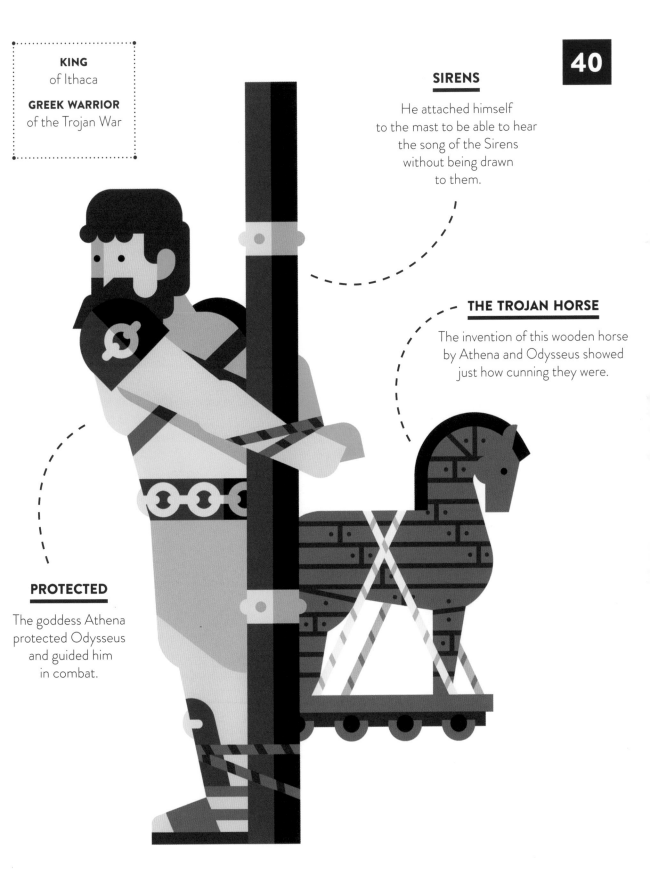

KING
of Ithaca

GREEK WARRIOR
of the Trojan War

SIRENS

He attached himself
to the mast to be able to hear
the song of the Sirens
without being drawn
to them.

THE TROJAN HORSE

The invention of this wooden horse
by Athena and Odysseus showed
just how cunning they were.

PROTECTED

The goddess Athena
protected Odysseus
and guided him
in combat.

The hero of the *Odyssey*

ZEUS'S FAMILY

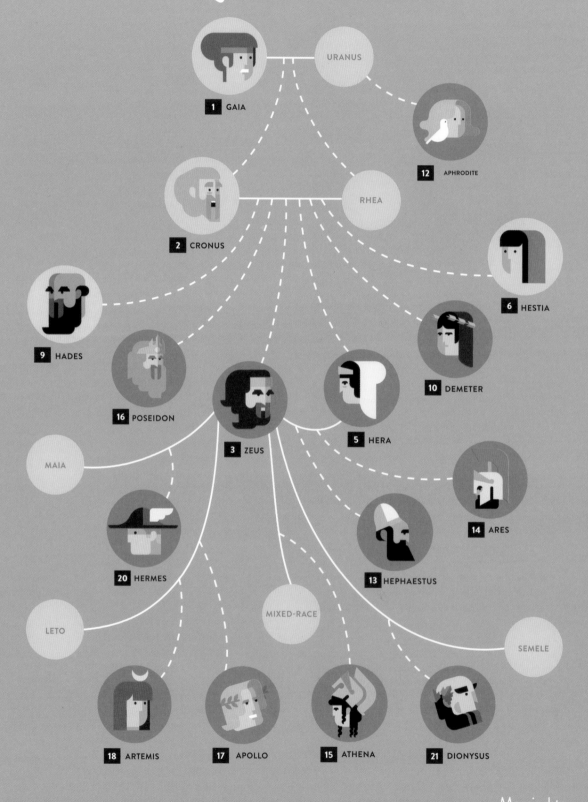

1 GAIA
URANUS
12 APHRODITE
2 CRONUS
RHEA
6 HESTIA
9 HADES
10 DEMETER
16 POSEIDON
3 ZEUS
5 HERA
MAIA
14 ARES
20 HERMES
13 HEPHAESTUS
LETO
MIXED-RACE
SEMELE
18 ARTEMIS
17 APOLLO
15 ATHENA
21 DIONYSUS

the 12 Olympians, gods who live on Mount Olympus

——— Married to...

- - - - - Child of...

THRACE

BLACK SEA

Mount Olympus
▲

Troy

THESSALY

ASIA
MINOR

AEGEAN SEA

LYDIA

PHOCIS

ITHACA

Delphi

Thebes

Aulis

ATTICA

Athens

Ephesus

Corinth

Mycenae

Epidaurus

PELOPONNESE

Argos

Olympia

NAXOS

Sparta

MEDITERRANEAN SEA

CRETE

ANCIENT GREECE

Inspiring | Educating | Creating | Entertaining

Brimming with creative inspiration, how-to projects, and useful information to enrich your everyday life, Quarto Knows is a favorite destination for those pursuing their interests and passions. Visit our site and dig deeper with our books into your area of interest: Quarto Creates, Quarto Cooks, Quarto Homes, Quarto Lives, Quarto Drives, Quarto Explores, Quarto Gifts, or Quarto Kids.

ISBN 978-1-78603-143-3

The illustrations were created digitally
Set in Brandon Grotesque and Gotham Rounded

Manufactured in Guangdong, China CC0518

9 8 7 6 5 4 3 2 1